Who the Hell is Karl Marx?

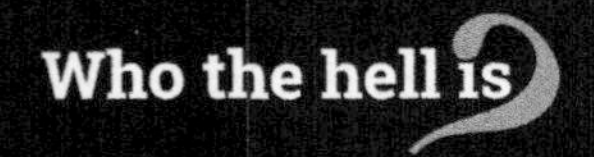
Who the hell is

Who the Hell is Karl Marx?

And what are his theories all about?

Manus McGrogan

First published in Great Britain in 2020 by
Bowden & Brazil Ltd
Felixstowe, Suffolk, UK.

British Library Cataloguing-in-Publication Data
A CIP record for this book is available from The British Library.

ISBN 978-1-9999492-6-6

To find out more about other books and authors in this series,
visit www.whothehellis.co.uk

Contents

Introduction

Philosopher, economist, journalist, historian and 'revolutionist', Karl Marx was a legend in his lifetime and far beyond. He is one of the four most influential thinkers of the last two hundred years, along with Sigmund Freud, Charles Darwin and Albert Einstein. Marx quickly grasped whatever subject he turned his mind to and managed to synthesize broadly from the disciplines of economics, philosophy, history and literature. He produced works of such power and originality that he pushed the boundaries of human understanding and transformed the way in which we think about the world.

Marx left us with a corpus of writing that is unparalleled in its intellectual scope and depth. *The Economic and Philosophical Manuscripts*, *The Communist Manifesto* and *Capital* were touchstones in his lifetime and remain almost biblical in their impact. It is striking how each successive work by Marx – and his long-time associate Friedrich Engels – builds on and enriches the previous ones, allowing readers of these texts to assemble Marx's world view. One major work, *The German Ideology*, remained unpublished until 1932, appearing long after his death. Yet it is a seminal statement of Marx's 'materialist conception of history' – essentially that of working-class revolution.

In the 150 years since his death, Karl Marx has become universally known. But his ideas have equally been subject to distortion and misrepresentation. Marxism has been variously (and often unfairly or incorrectly) associated with the totalitarian Stalinist regimes of the former Eastern bloc, the guerilla struggles of Africa, Asia and Latin America, and even with social democracy (such as the Labour Party in the UK or Democrats in the USA) in the Western world.

Even in his lifetime, followers of Marx fought over the meaning of his words, to the extent that an exasperated Marx himself declared that 'All I know is that I am no Marxist!' Yet a careful examination of their work shows that Marx and Engels provided very succinct definitions and understandings of the central concepts of 'class struggle', 'revolution' and 'communism', which are explored in full in this book.

Marx produced an enormous volume of work that probed into the distant past to uncover patterns of social change, wrote copiously about the events and movements of the 19th century, and forecast some of the major developments of the future, notably economic crisis, war and revolution.

We should not speak of Marx and his oeuvre without acknowledging the contribution of his friend and co-thinker Engels, writer and activist in his own right. It is debatable how much Marx would have achieved without the philosophical and material input of Engels. Although Marx's contribution to theory and knowledge was the greater, their partnership was indispensable to his formidable achievements.

This book traces the life of Marx, from his boisterous youth through his student years, before he emerged as the foremost leftist/radical writer, thinker and political activist of his time. It also outlines the seminal influences on Marx, and his absorption of philosophical, political and economic theory from the German, French and British thinkers of the 18th and 19th centuries.

The book then examines Marx's most important ideas, which were so potent and resilient that they apply as much today as they did in his era. Firstly, class struggle: the division of human civilization into warring socio-economic classes. For Marx and Engels, class struggle was the motive force of history, driving social change, and periodically exploding into revolutions that would usher in a new era of human 'progress'. We then explore some of Marx's key critiques of capitalism: the exploitation of the worker at the heart of the system, and the anarchic drive for profit that would doom the capitalist system to crisis. Lastly, we consider communism, the system that Marx envisaged would replace capitalism and end class society. What were the processes that he believed could free the mass of working people and bring about a new and equal society?

Time after time, authorities and ruling parties have declared Marx's ideas dead and defunct, and yet they continue to inform public debate. In the aftermath of the 2008 economic crisis, sales of T*he Communist Manifesto* and *Capital* soared. Marx's current German publisher, Jörn Schütrumpf of Karl- Dietz Publishing, said that new readers who were flocking to buy the books were typically 'those of a young academic generation, who have come to recognize that the neoliberal promises of happiness have not proved to be true' (*The Guardian*, 2008). Marx was the first to explicitly de-couple capitalist consumerism and happiness and reveal the inevitable boom-bust of capitalist economies, as he expertly analyzed both class struggle and economic crises. In today's political climate, his ideas are as vital and relevant as perhaps never before.

1. Marx's Life Story

Karl Marx was born on 5 May 1818 in the town of Trier, a city on the banks of the river Moselle in the Rhine province of Prussia (now known as Germany). He was the eldest son in a middle-class Jewish family, whose wealth acted to protect them a little from the anti-Semitism of the time. Karl's father, Heinrich Marx, was a successful lawyer, whose strong political ideas owed much both to the rationalism of the Enlightenment, and to the philosophers Immanuel Kant (1724–1804) and Voltaire (1694–1778). Karl's mother, Henrietta Pressburg, was from Holland, and like her husband was descended from a long line of rabbis.

The area in which the family lived when Karl was born had been through turbulent times, and was at that time ruled by Frederick Wilhelm III as an absolute monarch (meaning that he ruled without restraint of law or any governing body – parliament existed merely to rubber-stamp his edicts). The king reigned over a patchwork of provinces stretching from Poland to Alsace-Lorraine in France and he enforced his autocratic rule through suppression of political opposition, a network of police spies and censorship.

Significantly, the Rhineland region, and within it the Marxs' home town of Trier, had been annexed by France during the

Napoleonic wars. Under French rule, the citizens of Trier came to enjoy a measure of press freedom and religious tolerance; Jews were emancipated, just as they had been in France. But with the restoration of Prussian absolutism under Frederick Wilhelm III, anti-Semitic edicts were issued, barring Jews from public office and a number of professions. The Marx family was directly affected, as this discrimination barred Heinrich from practising as a lawyer. Having petitioned the authorities in vain for a lifting of the law, he converted to the Evangelical Church of Prussia, changing his name from his birth name of Herschel Levi to 'Heinrich' in the process.

At the age of six, Karl too was baptized; he was educated at home by Heinrich until the age of 10. The Trier secondary school he attended in his teens was staffed by liberal teachers. Heinrich's struggles with anti-Semitism, and the discussion of liberal, emancipatory ideas in the family and at school were not lost on the young Karl. He absorbed all of it at an early age, becoming an implacable opponent of the Prussian monarchy and quickly outstripping his own father's impulse for social change.

Karl was a boisterous child, developing an argumentative personality. According to his childhood friend Jenny von Westphalen, who later became his wife, Karl was 'domineering'. At school he was not noted for academic excellence, yet developed an interest in philosophy and literature. Moving to Bonn at the age of 17 to attend university, Marx led a rowdy, drunken lifestyle. He was even gaoled for 24 hours for being riotously drunk. While in Bonn, Marx attended a poets' society which doubled as a club for political dissidents. Occasionally he got into spats with the reactionary Borussia Korps, an aristocratic student fraternity. The following year one quarrel with a member of the Korps led to a duel, in which Marx was slightly wounded. The young man's antagonistic behaviour belied his fragile physical condition, which saw him being excused from military service after turning 18.

University and Young Hegelianism

In the summer of 1836, back in Trier, Karl secretly became engaged to Jenny, the daughter of Ludwig von Westphalen, an aristocratic Prussian official who had a deep interest in French liberalism and socialism. He encouraged his daughter to value ideals, find a progressive cause to which she could commit, and dedicate herself to fighting for it. Unsurprisingly both Jenny and the sympathetic Baron took a shine to the idealistic young man, and the Baron and Marx enjoyed walking and talking together. He shared with Marx an interest of philosophy and poetry, and instilled in him a lifelong love of Shakespeare. Jenny saw in Marx the romantic attributes of fictional characters she admired. To her, he was 'Goethe's Wilhelm Meister and Schiller's Karl von Moor, and he would be Shelley's Prometheus, chained to a precipice because he dared to challenge a tyrannical god' (Gabriel 2011). Marx himself had prefaced his dissertation

Fig. 1 Jenny von Westphalen, date unknown.

with a declaration of support for Prometheus, agreeing with his 'hatred of all heavenly and earthly gods who do not acknowledge human self-consciousness as the highest divinity' (Stedman Jones, 2016).

However, other, more reactionary members of the Westphalen family did not look kindly on Marx, because it was far outside the cultural norms for an aristocratic young woman to marry a Jewish radical. Fearing their families' disapproval, Karl and Jenny became secretly engaged, and were married in 1843, when Karl was 25 and Jenny 29. Both their fathers were happy about the union, but sadly neither lived long enough to witness the wedding.

In the autumn of 1836, just a few months after becoming engaged, Marx transferred to the prestigious University of Berlin to continue his studies in law. He spent as much time writing verse, influenced by the German satirical poet and distant cousin Heinrich Heine. As this stage the young Marx aspired to become a poet and playwright himself. He attempted to realize this dream while at University where, amidst his law studies, he wrote several dramatic pieces. However, recognizing that his writing (and ideas) borrowed too heavily from other great authors, such as Johann Goethe (1749–1832) and Laurence Sterne (1713–68), he eventually abandoned his literary ambitions. He decided instead to throw himself fully into the study of philosophy, at a time when intellectual life in Germany was thriving.

It was in Berlin that Marx encountered the ideas of the late Georg Wilhelm Friedrich Hegel (1770–1831), the most influential Prussian thinker of the age. Initially repelled by Hegel's writing style, Marx was gradually converted to the philosopher's thought and methods. He was particularly taken with Hegel's method of the dialectic, which claimed to explain how ideas evolve. Hegel claimed that an idea (thesis) always contains within it a contradiction (antithesis), instigating a conflict that would ultimately lead to the evolution of a new idea that contained both the thesis and antithesis, and in this way solve the problem of contradiction (see Chapter 2). It was an intellectual thunderbolt in the 19-year-old's life, which turned him from his law studies and set him on the path of radical philosophy.

Subsequently, Marx joined a group of free thinkers dubbed the 'Young Hegelians', who exalted Hegel's method while rejecting his political conservatism. Among their number were the philosophy lecturer Bruno Bauer (1809–82) and philosopher and political writer Arnold Ruge (1802–80). In taking up with this group, Marx resumed a lifestyle of drinking and lively debate with like-minded thinkers. However, this turn of events was not to the liking of Heinrich Marx, who berated his son's profligacy when he ought to have been diligently pursuing his studies and a future career in law. His mother too would berate Karl for failing to observe a more Spartan lifestyle. But Karl simply ignored his parents' advice, just as he lost interest in returning to Trier to see family and fiancée. In fact, he became so preoccupied with the Young Hegelians and his new doctoral thesis that in 1838 he even missed his father's death and funeral. With his mother now in control of the family finances, her frequently penniless son would often write to her requesting sums of money.

In 1840, Friedrich Wilhelm IV acceded to the throne and autocratic rule in the country was tightened still further. The Young Hegelians' attempts to influence the intellectual scene at Berlin University dissipated as a new wave of conservative professors was appointed. Bauer was exiled from the University, and Marx did not bother to return to classes in Berlin, especially as the philosophy department was now run by an anti-Hegelian, Friedrich von Schelling (1775–1854). However, he continued to work on his thesis – on Greek materialist philosophy – and eventually submitted it to the University of Jena. He was awarded a doctorate on the basis of the work's scholarly rigour. The publication in 1841 of *The Essence of Christianity* by the Berlin philosopher Ludwig Feuerbach (1804–72) deeply impressed Marx and his friends. Feuerbach rejected Hegel's notions of divine superiority, instead arguing that God was no more than a human projection, cast by humans living in the real, material world. There was no other 'ideal' world, according to Feuerbach, nor any god. It was this materialism, allied to Hegel's dialectical method that now began to drive forward Marx's philosophy.

The path was not straightforward, though, and controversy continued to follow Marx. A short stay in Bonn with his friend Bauer, newly appointed at the University there, culminated in their joint writing of a satirical pamphlet on Hegel, which served to earn Bauer yet another expulsion.

Editing the News

Marx decided to swap the drink and politics circuit of Bonn and Berlin for that of Cologne in Rhineland Germany. The most industrially advanced and politically progressive city in Prussia, Cologne nurtured an urban merchant and manufacturing class, or 'bourgeoisie', which lobbied for a greater say in the affairs of the country. Marx's arrival in the city coincided with the founding of the newspaper that best reflected liberal bourgeois interests, the *Rheinische Zeitung*. It was not long before he was writing for the paper. Around this time he penned a brilliant essay against censorship for the Young Hegelian journal *Deutsche Jahrbücher*. Ironically, it was immediately banned by the authorities.

At the *Rheinische Zeitung* he made an immediate impression on the resident intellectuals, among them the paper's radical editor Arnold Rutenberg, and lead writer Moses Hess, a communist. In the 'Doctor's Club', home of Cologne's intelligentsia, members were awestruck by Marx's intellectual prowess, force of conviction and hirsute appearance. He was described in a friend's poem as that 'swarthy chap from Trier' (Callinicos, 2010). Thick black hair sprouted from his head and cheeks, earning him the nickname 'Moor', and adding to his aura of philosophical gravitas.

Marx's first articles were powerful attacks on Prussian absolutism and the ineptitude of the liberal opposition, and quickly led to his promotion as editor of the *Rheinische Zeitung*. Under his stewardship the paper's circulation and reputation quickly grew. Politically, Marx was now a radical liberal democrat, who wanted to see universal suffrage. He was also interested in new socialist and communist ideas, of social equality and communal property, but was hesitant to subscribe to them.

Even so, Marx's study of relations between the state, property and class was taking him in a more radical direction. In particular his analysis and critique of a new law on wood theft led him to see the ways in which the state acted to protect the interests of the rich and powerful. Marx's socialist worldview was beginning to take shape. During this time he became increasingly estranged from Bauer and the Young Hegelians. He refuted their extreme

Fig. 2 Marx and Engels at the Rheinische Zeitung, 1849

idealism, while they denounced his editorial compromises with Prussian censors. Yet Marx had little choice but to accede to some of the censors' demands simply to keep the Rheinische Zeitung in circulation. Even with these compromises, Marx failed to stem the state's censorial intentions and he left the paper shortly before it was banned in summer 1843.

Marx in Paris

Seeking respite from the relentless struggle against absolutism in Germany, Marx moved to Paris with his wife in October 1843. The plan was to establish a new *Deutsche Jahrbücher* with his friend and fellow German émigré Arnold Ruge. For a while they shared a communal dwelling in rue Vaneau with Ruge and other German exiles, but conditions were hard. Shortly after moving out, Jenny gave birth to their first child, who was named Jenny after her mother, although called 'Jennychen' by family and close friends.

Although France was ruled by the reactionary monarchy of Louis Philippe, the climate in the French capital was conducive to radicalism. The country had been shaken by revolutions over the previous 50 years and the capital played host to a variety of underground activists and thinkers. In the secret societies such as the 'League of the Just', Marx met and debated with the French utopian socialist Victor Considerant (1808–93) and the anarchists Pierre-Joseph Proudhon (1809–65) from France and Mikhail Bakunin (1814–76) from Russia. Anarchism was a political philosophy that opposed authority and hierarchy, and advocated self-managed societies. Marx was impressed by Proudhon's work *What is Property?* (1840), which called for the abolition of private property. Marx also met with French and émigré German workers, whom he eulogized for their rebel spirit. The working class had started to move centre stage in Marx's thinking.

It was in Paris that Marx met and befriended the German philosopher Friedrich Engels (1820–95). A former member of the Berlin liberal intelligentsia and Young Hegelians, Engels was a talented writer and journalist who had also lived and worked in Manchester at his family's textile firm. This experience would lead him to produce significant critical studies of British industrial capitalism and the condition of British workers, which strongly impressed Marx.

By different routes, Marx and Engels were coming to similar conclusions about the role of the working class and its potential for revolution. They struck up a partnership of ideas and writing, beginning a lifelong collaboration that started with a stinging attack on Bruno Bauer and the increasingly idealist and abstract Young Hegelians.

Marx still believed that a revolution would require the leadership of enlightened thinkers. But his view of the working class as a passive force for change began to take a different direction. In an article entitled 'On the Jewish question', published in the short-lived *Deutsch-Französische Jahrbücher* in 1844, Marx argued for a revolution in social relations and not simply in government. And in another essay he called for just such a revolution in Prussia, believing that only the German working class possessed the necessary force to overthrow Prussian tyranny.

Marx then turned his attention to economics in his critical evaluation of the work of economists Adam Smith (1723–90) and David Ricardo (1772–1823), concluding that workers were compelled to revolt by their very role as producers within capitalism. When a weavers' strike broke out in Silesia in 1844, Marx pointed to their high level of organization and consciousness as evidence that workers could act independently and in their own interest.

The Road to Revolution

Marx's prominence in the Parisian radical scene brought the outspoken German to the attention of the French authorities. In February 1845 he was expelled from France. In debt for unpaid rent, Jenny sold all their furniture, and the young family set off for Brussels. Marx hoped to be able to think and act more freely in Belgium, where he was soon joined by Engels.

Marx and Engels were soon on an intellectual offensive again, attacking the Young Hegelian anarchist Max Stirner's (1806–56) ode to individualism. In the Spring of 1846, they wrote their seminal work *The German Ideology*, outlining the theoretical cornerstone of their revolutionary socialism – historical materialism – which asserts that history is shaped by the material development of human society.

For Marx and Engels, theory could no longer be divorced from practice, and they threw themselves into political activity. They went to London, and explored the industrial slums of Manchester, gathering information on the economical and political life of the English working class. Jenny, meanwhile, was pregnant with a second child, Laura, but was equally focused on an injustice. She wrote letters to Marx about the difficulties that women suffered at all levels of society, and the inequality of the rights in comparison to men. She knew that he was working on a book – *The German Ideology* – but not that the work had stalled. With the family's finances already in dire straits, and the birth of Laura in September 1845, Marx withheld this fact from his wife as he continued his ideological journey with Engels.

Their chosen terrain was the League of the Just, an organization split between the ideas of the French revolutionary Louis Auguste Blanqui (1805–81), who believed that only an elite could forcibly take power on behalf of the masses, and other political thinkers who held to a peaceful road to socialism.

Marx and Engels fought their own corner by setting up the Communist Correspondence Committee, a network of activist groups in the various European capitals that could provide information to one another and exchange ideas. Jenny worked as their secretary, taking part in their discussions, deciphering Marx's illegible handwriting, and organizing events. By June 1847, they had succeeded in winning control of the League of the Just, transforming the organization into the Communist

League. Jenny became the group's first member, having given birth to the couple's third child, Edgar, four months earlier. Marx and Engels were then commissioned to write a statement of the League's principles. The result was *The Communist Manifesto*, a public declaration of their revolutionary ideas. It was to become the most famous of all socialist pamphlets, ending with the declaration: 'Workers of the world unite!'

The *Manifesto* was prescient. Within a year, revolutions had broken out across Europe, beginning in France in February 1848. These were national, democratic upheavals, revolts against monarchies and authoritarian regimes. Both the liberal bourgeoisie and the working classes of the continent were involved – the former with demands for the vote, the latter against poverty and unemployment. But whereas the liberals saw representative government within the nation state as the end goal, the working classes wanted to go further still. They were determined to challenge the ruling orders to go beyond and challenge capitalism.

Marx had been granted asylum in Belgium on condition that he refrain from political activity, but as revolutions broke out in 1848, he broke that promise both journalistically and by gathering weapons for German revolutionaries. He and Jenny were arrested and immediately exiled from Belgium. They dashed first to Paris, where the French monarchy had just collapsed, before travelling on to Cologne and German unrest. Prussian censorship had subsided, and Marx quickly took control of the newspaper *Neue Rheinische Zeitung*. At the helm of the new paper he was much better placed to influence events, especially as the League was too small to intervene in the movement.

At this point Marx and Engels still believed that the German workers should follow the liberal bourgeoisie in the revolt against absolutism, and argued accordingly in the paper. Even so, Marx took note of the growing 'civil war' between labour and capital in France, where a worker's uprising in June 1848 was crushed by the bourgeois republican government. Over the next year the authorities harried the editors of the *Neue Rheinische Zeitung* for the venom of their oppositional articles. Indeed, in January 1849, Marx was taken to court for allegedly 'insulting the public prosecutor', but was cleared after a rousing speech in his own defence. He made no apologies from the dock, saying, 'It is the duty of the press to come forward on behalf of the oppressed in its immediate neighbourhood...The first duty of the press is to undermine all the foundations of the existing political state of affairs' (Wheen 1999).

Marx's acquittal proved insufficient to stop the hounding of the *Neue Rheinische Zeitung*, and the authorities effectively killed off the paper by indicting one section of the staff and expelling the rest from the country. Leaving Engels to continue the fight in defence of the republican Palatinate (an area of southwestern Germany), Marx again fled to Paris, where he found that the revolution had drawn to a close. His family travelled to Paris to join him, but no sooner had they arrived than he was once more given his marching orders by the French government, and on 23 August was told that he must leave within 24 hours.

London: *Das Kapital*

Three days after his deportation from France, Marx arrived in London, where he was joined by his family a month later. He began organizing the work of the Communist League's Central

Authority and set up a Committee of Support for German Political Refugees. In November 1849 Jenny gave birth to their fourth child, Heinrich Guido, and around five days later Engels arrived in London. It was an exile that they all expected to be brief, and at first Marx and Engels were preoccupied with reviving the Communist League. They shared a belief with the followers of Blanqui in the imminent revival of revolution. At the same time, they denounced the continuing Blanquist calls for the armed overthrow of the state by an enlightened minority on behalf of the people. Marx and Engels founded a new journal, the *Neue Rheinische Zeitung* Revue that could serve as a rallying point for German socialists and political refugees in London. In the newspaper Marx wrote an analysis of the 1848 revolutions that was published as 'The Class Struggle in France'.

Yet there would be no renewal of the revolutionary ferment. By the early 1850s authoritarian regimes prevailed in France and Germany, and the revolutionary émigrés could not look to workers in Britain where the class struggle was at low ebb.

Marx recognized as much, seeing the prospects of revolution dimmed by capitalist expansion. Much as the economic crisis of the 1840s had exacerbated the contradictions in European societies and provoked revolution, so economic prosperity in the 1850s had stabilized these societies. Marx's studies led him to conclude that revolution was not possible under the circumstances. His political hopes collapsed.

This pessimistic outlook provoked angry reactions from others in the League, prompting Marx and Engels to leave the organization. Marx disliked the bickering émigré scene, filled as it was with preening poets and self-important radicals of the European revolutionary diaspora. He would often take the 'democratic simpletons' to task in his letters and writings, and even challenged several to duels (unfought) over baseless accusations or straightforward insults. Although he was among the most ardent champions of embattled revolutionaries back home, Marx made a sport of verbally skewering his rivals and fellow émigrés, revealing a biting wit that would serve him well during the difficult London years.

During the 1850s, Marx effectively withdrew from political activity and focused on writing. He wrote another political essay, on the authoritarian Louis-Napoleon's coup in France, and then resumed his economic studies in the British Library, where he would spend days on research and writing. His work during this time laid the foundations for what would become his masterwork *Das Kapital* (Capital). Through this in-depth, detailed analysis of the workings of capitalism he aimed to uncover the dynamics and contradictions of the system.

The decade proved a grim time for the Marx family. They were forced to abandon their former 'bourgeois' comforts, moving between cramped homes in Soho, constantly in debt to local shopkeepers, and increasingly reliant on donations from Engels, who had moved back to Manchester to work at the family firm. Between 1850–55 three of the Marx children died – two at the age of only a year old, and Edgar at the age of eight. The family were so impoverished that Jenny was forced to beg £2.00 from a neighbour to pay for one of the children's coffins.

Home life had become intolerably hard. Both Marx and Jenny were suffering tremendous grief in addition to financial hardship, and the loss, for Marx, of his political hopes. In a letter to Engels in 1851, Marx wrote: 'Am annoyed and enraged by streams of tears all night long…I'm sorry for my wife. She bears the brunt of the pressure, and au fond she is right. In spite of this…from time to time I lose my temper' (Marx to Engels, 31 July 1851).

During this time of intense pressure, Marx had a child by his loyal family servant, Helene Demuth. The affair was hushed up and kept secret even from Jenny. The ever-faithful Engels took responsibility for the parentage, and the child, born in 1851 and named Henry Frederick, was placed in foster care. It showed that Marx tried to maintain a veneer of family respectability, despite grinding poverty, and was not immune from the hypocrisies of bourgeois life. This seems also to have been true of later Communist authorities, as the documentation about the child was ordered to be 'buried in the archive' by Stalin himself in 1934 (Kapp, 1994). Nonetheless, Demuth continued to stay in the household, as housekeeper, and would be buried in the Marx family grave when she died.

The decade was dire for the Marxes, and yet the report of one Prussian spy from their Dean Street home in 1852 painted a picture of cheery hospitality amid their wretched circumstances:

> *'As father and husband, Marx, in spite of his wild and restless character, is the gentlest and mildest of men… Everything is dirty, and covered with dust…Here is a chair with only three legs…but none of these things embarrass Marx or his wife…You are received in the most friendly way…Finally you grow accustomed to the company and find it interesting and original.'* (Callinicos 2010)

Speaking only a little English, Marx struggled to find work. By now he had another mouth to feed after the birth of a daughter, Jenny Julia Eleanor, known as 'Tussy'. He wrote articles and reports for the progressive *New York Daily Tribune* and other, bourgeois papers, translated from the German by Wilhelm Pieper. In 1858 Marx completed a lengthy outline of his economic writings, later published as *Grundrisse* (Fundamentals). At the same time, the world economy now re-entered a period of crisis, raising the hopes of Marx, Engels and the radicals everywhere that revolution could begin anew. The failure of said revolution to materialize took Marx back to his treatise on capitalism, of which *Grundrisse* was intended merely as a draft preface to a main section entitled 'Economics'. His plan was to write six volumes on various interconnected economic aspects: capital; landed property; wage labour; the State; trade, and the world market. Following prolonged study in the British Library, the title was revised to *Capital* and the content re-divided into four volumes on production, distribution, capitalism and surplus value.

Fig. 3 Karl Marx, 1861

Capital took another eight years of toil, during which time he and his family continued to survive on handouts from Engels or other friends (he also received some money from his mother).

Marx would often write in pain and discomfort, afflicted by boils and carbuncles. He stated that he had sacrificed 'health happiness and family' in the pursuit of *Capital*. Finally, in 1858, Volume 1 of *Capital* was published in German. In later years, Marx's daughters made fun of Jenny's habit of reading the book so often, but Marx said that the most important thing about its publication was that he received it in time 'so that my dear wife had the last days of her life still cheered up. You know the passionate interest she took in all such affairs' (Marx to F. A. Sorge, 15 Dec 1881).

Twilight Years

In 1862 the American Civil War put an end to Marx's income from American newspapers, and Marx at one point even applied to become a clerk with the Great Western Railway. His illegible handwriting earned him a rejection, and the Marxes lurched from one financial crisis to another until Engels paid off all their debts and assured Marx of an annuity of £350. While Marx's enormous capacity for reading never faltered, he was now much less prolific in his writing. This was in part because his health continued to decline. Having endured years of liver and gall-bladder disease attacks, and constant boils and abscesses, in 1873, he suffered a partial stroke. The ensuing years were dogged by headaches, insomnia, inflammation of the eyes, neuralgia, rheumatic pains and recurring bronchitis. Ill-health prompted several treatments in the German spa of Karlsbad in the mid-1870s.

Marx and his wife were able to spend their final years in relative comfort, owing to the generosity of Engels, who also moved to London and whose home became a hub for radical activities.

Two of the Marx daughters married socialists of the French Communard diaspora in London, Laura to Paul Lafargue and Jenny to Charles Longuet. The bourgeois in Marx had reservations about the French socialists, as their job prospects were bleak and he feared for his daughters' welfare. And he was especially critical of his third daughter Eleanor's liaison with Commune historian Prosper Lissagaray; the domineering father was possessive of his youngest, as well as selfishly reliant on her assistance in his late scientific research.

In his twilight years Marx came to lean more on his family for emotional solace. Then in 1881, his wife Jenny died of cancer, leaving him disconsolate. He took several vacations to lift his ailing spirits but was further anguished by the death of his eldest child, Jenny, in January 1883. Physically exhausted and emotionally drained, Marx himself died two months later, on 14 March. He was laid to rest in London's Highgate Cemetery, the plinth carrying some of his more famous quotations. Engels spoke eloquently at his graveside:

> *'An immeasurable loss has been sustained both by the militant proletariat of Europe and America, and by historical science, in the death of this man. The gap that has been left by the departure of this mighty spirit will soon enough make itself felt.'* (*Der Sozialdemokrat*, 22 March 1883)

Karl Marx's Timeline

Karl Marx		World Events	
1818	Karl Heinrich Marx is born in Trier, Prussia (now Germany)		
		1830-31	Revolutions in France and Belgium, uprisings in Poland
		1832	A mass political demonstration (The Hambach Festivities) demands the unification of Germany and political freedoms
1836	Marx enrols at Berlin University as a law student; becomes a member of the Young Hegelians		
1837	Marx begins to study Hegel's philosophy		
		1838	Chartism, the first mass revolutionary workers' movement, emerges in England
		1840	Proudhon publishes *What is Property?*
1842	Marx becomes editor-in-chief at *Rheinische Zeitung*; meets Engels for the first time		
1843	Marx marries Jenny von Westphalen. They move to Paris where their first child Jennychen is born	1843	Prussian Government bans the *Rheinische Zeitung*
1844	Marx begins work on ***Economic and Philosophic Manuscripts***, criticizing bourgeois political economy	1844	Weaver's strike breaks out in Silesia
1845	Following pressure from Prussia, France orders Marx to leave. Moves with his family to Brussels where their second child, Laura is born	1845	Engels publishes *The Condition of the Working Class in England*
1846	Marx and Engels write ***The German Ideology***, which isn't published until 1932		
1847	Marx's ***Poverty of Philosophy*** is published in French in Brussels. Jenny gives birth to their third child, Edgar		
1848	Marx and Jenny exiled from Belgium; travel to Germany where Marx takes control of *Neue Rheinische Zeitung*	1848	Revolutionary events flare up in Vienna and Berlin as well as in Hungary, France and Italy
1849	Authorities close *Neue Rheinische Zeitung*; Marx returns to Paris, then on to London; Jenny gives birth to their fourth child, Heinrich	1849	Corn Laws abolished in Britain
1850	Marx and Engels write pamphlet, **'The Great Men of the Exile'**; Marx's son, Heinrich dies		

1851 Jenny gives birth to their fifth child, Franziska, who dies a year later

1853 The *Chartist People's Paper* prints a series of Marx's articles

1854 Marx writes letter to the Labour Parliament in *The People's Paper*, calling for establishment of a mass working-class political party in England.

1855 Jenny gives birth to their sixth child, Tussy

1857 Marx's articles on crisis in Europe and USA appear in American, British and German press

1857 Worldwide economic crisis

1859 ***A Contribution to the Critique of Political Economy*** is published

1861 American Civil War breaks out

1867 Volume I of ***Das Kapital*** is published

1871 Proletarian revolution in Paris; Commune established

1873 Marx suffers partial stroke

1881 Marx's wife, Jenny, dies in London after a long illness

1883 Marx dies in London and is buried in Highgate Cemetary

1885 Volume II of ***Das Kapital***, edited by Engels, is published

1894 Volume III of ***Das Kapital***, edited by Engels, is published

2. Influences on Marx's Thinking

Throughout his life, Marx drew on the ideas of a myriad of writers and thinkers. His body of works was built through relentless reading and absorption of the greatest philosophers and economists, and the testing of ideas against scientific enquiry and developments in the real world. Through his critical revision of others' ideas he established new ideas, concepts and arguments.

Marx drew on three main intellectual sources, primarily of the 18th and 19th centuries: German (idealist) philosophy, French (utopian) socialism and British (bourgeois) economics. It was on these foundations that he constructed – in collaboration with Engels – his philosophy of historical materialism, and expounded his ideas on capitalism and socialism. He was equally influenced by the momentous events of his lifetime, which often served to confirm or deny his theoretical writings. The 1848 revolutions in Europe, in particular, impacted on both his intellectual development and his personal situation.

German Idealism

Marx's theory of historical materialism was rooted in his study and critique of Germany philosophy, in particular the work of Hegel and Feuerbach. Materialism was a concept derived from ancient Greek philosophy stemming from the thought of atomists such as Democritus and Epicurus. It acquired its name because these philosophers believed that everything in the world is made up of matter; specifically, of indivisible particles that they called 'atoms'. It was the first philosophical approach that seemed to solve the problem of how one thing changes into another. The atomists said that as atoms combined or disconnected in various ways, change in the overall structure of the thing (such as a plant) could be seen. Marx made a comparative study of these two ancient philosophers in his later doctoral thesis, favouring Epicurus, who also introduced the idea that atoms could 'swerve' and that this accounted for their being attracted to or repulsed from each other. This ability meant that it was not possible to have an entirely deterministic view of what might happen; it allowed for unexpected change. Marx noted in his dissertation that 'the declination breaks the bonds of fate' and when applied to human consciousness, 'the declination is that something in its breast that can fight back and resist'.

Engels continued Marx's work on Epicurus, and came to describe his ideas on change as 'immanent dialectics' (see 'Hegel' below). Marx was also admiring of Epicurus's stand against the power of religion, and in 1841 wrote his dissertation on Democritus and Epicurus. Marx and Engels summed up their reasons for admiration in *The German Ideology*:

> *'Epicurus... was the true radical Enlightener of antiquity; he openly attacked the ancient religion, and it was from him, too, that the atheism of the Romans,*

> *insofar as it existed, was derived. For this reason... among all church fathers, from Plutarch to Luther, Epicurus has always had the reputation of being the atheist philosopher par excellence, and was called a swine.'* (Marx & Engels 1845)

Hegel

While in Berlin during the late 1830s, Marx threw himself into the study of philosophy, at a time when intellectual life in Germany was flourishing. He soon came to grips with the ideas of the most influential philosopher of the age, (the late) Georg Hegel.

Hegel saw things in nature not as fixed, separate entities, but as interrelated and undergoing a process of birth, growth and decay. He believed that thought and the world were one and the same and that the world was essentially knowable. Moreover he believed that existence stemmed from a universal Spirit, or God. Yet this Spirit had become divorced from the world it had created. Hegel had also been influenced by the progressive ideas of the French Enlightenment, the 18th-century intellectual movement that championed the capacity of human reason to explain the world, as against the traditional, irrational and religious views of the past. He came to see human history – the unfolding of human reason – as the vehicle by which the world and Spirit could be reconciled. History was a process or development of interconnected ideas, moving towards the ultimate goal of the Spirit, also referred to as the 'Absolute', 'Idea', (or Divine Truth), in other words, God.

To explain the way in which ideas evolved, Hegel introduced the process of the 'dialectic', an ancient concept which suggested that opposing or contradictory elements within an idea, entity or state of affairs could be united to establish a new and higher idea. Another way to explain the dialectical process is to start with one idea (or state of affairs) and name this 'the thesis'. An idea that contradicts the thesis is known as 'the antithesis'. When these two contradictory ideas combine, the result is that the thesis is negated, and a new idea (or state of affairs) arises. This is known as 'the synthesis'. However, as with the original idea, the synthesis, once established, is also found wanting and seen to contain contradictions, beginning the process – or 'dialectic' – all over again.

Like the Ancient Greek atomists, Hegel was also studying change, but he suggested that progress is based on the dialectic; it is built on the fact that all ideas contain within them contradictions, or opposites. They negate themselves. In this way, he said, nature undergoes a permanent process of change and transformation. History, too, proceeds by a process of contradiction and resolution. Moreover, when a thing negates itself it is turned into its opposite. Hegel argued that quantity was turned into quality, by which he meant that change would take place gradually before dramatic, qualitative leaps to a different state.

One manifestation in the physical world is the way that water is able to shift between different states. When heat is applied to water, the liquid gradually warms up before reaching boiling point and then, suddenly, converts to steam. The water is 'negated', becoming its opposite, steam. Quantitative change gives way to qualitative.

This model of historical transformation led Hegel earlier in his life to favour social and political progress, and he welcomed the French Revolution and the Napoleonic conquest of Prussia. But he later grew reactionary and came to see the Prussian Absolutist State as the highest state of human endeavour and embodiment of reason.

Marx was at first repelled by Hegel's awkward writing style. 'I did not care for its grotesque and rocky melody', he said (McLellan 1983). But in an intense period of writing and reflection in Berlin, he found himself irrevocably drawn to the 'Hegelian system' or dialectical method. Marx was eternally indebted to Hegel. He and Engels would come to apply the dialectic in their theory of historical materialism, showing how each phase of social evolution contained the germ of its own revolutionary transformation, with movement towards the endpoint of communism, the highest state of human society.

Marx was also influenced by the 'Young Hegelians' (sometimes 'Left Hegelians') at University, a radical philosophical group that sought to apply Hegel's negationist dialectic to religion and politics. Among the Berlin members of this group was Bruno Bauer, an early intellectual mentor of Marx who had studied under Hegel; Arnold Ruge, who edited the radical journal *Deutsche Jahrbucher*; and Max Stirner, whose work acted as a forerunner to existentialism, individualist anarchism and psychoanalytic theory. Marx and Engels were also members of the group, which was regularly spied upon by a 'secret policeman' who reported the group's activities to the authorities. The presence of the policeman was documented in a cartoon by Engels (see below). The Young Hegelians substituted Hegel's ideal of the Absolute (divine) with that of humanity. But while they agreed with Hegel that the State embodied reason, they opposed the reactionary Prussian state in favour of a liberal democracy.

Fig. 4 Cartoon by Friedrich Engels of *Die Freien*, the Berlin section of the Young Hegelians, c. 1842.

Hegel had unveiled the dialectical process in nature and history. He also believed that 'thought' preceded and created material reality – that God created the Earth, and humankind. But another Young Hegelian thinker, Ludwig Feuerbach, saw things differently. Thought, argued Feuerbach, was a product of the human brain, itself a part of the real, material world. As such, humans created God, not the other way around. God, or the 'Absolute' (in Hegel's terms), is simply a product of the human imagination. Furthermore, humans attributed to God all the best things they saw in humanity, such as kindness, mercy and love, together with humanity's own powers: the capacity to think, act and create. In so doing, they created a being that was all-powerful and perfect, and rendered themselves powerless.

Religion was therefore a form of alienation which prevented people from realizing their true nature, or 'species being', as Feuerbach called it.

In his work Feuerbach brought a materialist analysis to bear on the Hegelian method, publishing his core ideas in his book *The Essence of Christianity* (1841). Engels stated that having read it, 'we all became Feuerbachians overnight'. He went on, 'How enthusiastically Marx greeted the new interpretation, and how greatly – despite all critical reservations – he was influenced by it, we can read in "The Holy Family"' (Engels 1886).

However, Engels and Marx did not completely agree with Feuerbach, who believed that human's true nature was fixed (while Marx held in mind the quantum 'swerve' of atoms and their disruptive effect). Feuerbach believed that our fundamental human nature could only be grasped once the influence of religion had been removed, while Marx and Engels believed that, essentially, people needed to be educated out of religion. In the *Theses on Feuerbach* (1845), Marx argued that religion was the product of underlying social and economic relations in society and that its influence would only disappear once those relations had been irrevocably changed.

Feuerbach had also jettisoned Hegel's dialectic, whereas Marx sought to adopt the dialectic and liberate it from the realm of abstract and religious thought. In the Afterword to the second edition of *Das Kapital*, Marx wrote,

> *'My dialectic method is not only different from the Hegelian, but is its direct opposite. To Hegel, the life-process of the human brain, i.e. the process of*

> *thinking, which, under the name of "the Idea," he even transforms into an independent subject, is the demiurgos of the real world, and the real world is only the external, phenomenal form of "the Idea." With me, on the contrary, the ideal is nothing else than the material world reflected by the human mind, and translated into forms of thought.'* (Marx 1873)

But Marx pays homage to Hegel for having originated this powerful idea. Also in the same Afterword, Marx notes,

> *'The mystification which dialectic suffers in Hegel's hands, by no means prevents him from being the first to present its general form of working in a comprehensive and conscious manner. With him it is standing on its head. It must be turned right side up again, if you would discover the rational kernel within the mystical shell.'* (Marx, 1873)

Significantly, Marx saw productive activity as central to our species being, which meant that he saw it as fundamental to us as our biological, psychological and evolutionary aspects, such as our drives for food, sleep, sex, love, belonging and conformity. Marx saw productive activity as a social process, whereby we, as humans, transform nature and ourselves. But under capitalism, he saw that workers lost this sense of productive activity – the daily work that they actively undertook had been reduced to selling their skills and effort with no control over what they have produced, leaving them permanently unfulfilled. Humans experience a fourfold estrangement and alienation, Marx said: from the product of labour, from productive activity, from species being, and finally from other humans. To overcome this alienation requires a revolutionary transformation of the social relations, and attainment of a society of freedom and fulfilment: communism.

Marx's first encounter with communism as a political force came in Cologne at the *Rheinische Zeitung*, whose editor Adolf Rutenberg was a Hegelian, and its leading writer, Moses Hess, a communist. Marx had lively discussions with them as well as the other radicals in the Cologne Circle, and was entrusted the editorship of the paper in 1842. However, when the *Rheinische Zeitung* was accused of communist sympathies, Marx was evasive, writing: 'The *Rheinische Zeitung* [...] does not admit that communist ideas in their present form possess even theoretical reality, and therefore can still less desire their practical realization.' (Callinicos 2010)

Even so, the radicalism of his political environment was pushing Marx in the direction of socialism. While editor of the *Rheinische Zeitung* he was forced to write about the 'uninspiring debates' (Marx 1842) of the local authority on the theft of wood. He found himself in the 'embarrassing position of having to discuss what is known as material interests'. The 'wood theft' law was a measure introduced by the authorities to secure the Moselle landowners' holdings and punish the poor peasants of the area (who had stolen wood on the land). Marx's intense concern with the question added a crucial economic dimension to his hitherto political thought. He realized that the various classes had material, economic interests; indeed, the state was not a neutral bystander in the matter, but acted to defend the economic interests of the rich and powerful.

Utopian Socialism

The second major influence on Marx's ideas was that of French socialism. It was a radical tradition that grew out of the Great Revolution of 1789–99. Marx himself was fascinated by the French Revolution which he described as 'the most colossal revolution that history has ever known' (Marx & Engels 1976).

The Revolution had swept aside the monarchy and remnants of feudalism, clearing the path for capitalism, and its message had been carried to the four corners of Europe by Napoleon's armies.

Yet even during the Revolutionary years, some argued that the Revolution had failed to live up to its ideals of liberty, equality and fraternity. In 1797, the revolutionary François-Noël Babeuf (1760–1797), known as 'Gracchus', and the 'Conspiracy of Equals' attempted to restore the Jacobin dictatorship and impose a regime which would bring about equality and communal property. The conspiracy was crushed and Babeuf executed but his early socialist ideas persisted.

The 'utopians', so called by Marx and Engels because of their romantic, sometimes naïve vision of a perfect society, emerged in the decades after the Revolution. Foremost amongst them were Frenchmen Henri de Saint-Simon (1760–1825), Charles Fourier (1772–1837) and Etienne Cabet (1788–1856) and the Welshman Robert Owen (1771–1858). Both Marx and Engels were admirers and regularly cited their influence, Engels stating at one point that they should be considered among the greatest minds of all time.

Attacking the inequality and inhumanity of bourgeois society, the utopians proposed the model of a future world based on cooperation, efficient production and fair distribution of the material wealth.

Moreover, they advocated experiments in communal living and working whereby these principles could be applied.

The earliest of these, Saint-Simon, believed that the study of the past would teach humanity how to live in the future. Like Hegel and the Enlightenment thinkers, he saw human progress towards the victory of reason. But he also understood society as passing through different stages governed by different class systems and ideologies. Agrarian feudalism and monotheistic religion, as he saw it, were superseded by urban capitalism and scientific reason. In a real sense capitalism provided the basis of a new society founded on reason.

Saint-Simon also condemned the division of society by class, where the rich and powerful squeezed the masses; he spoke of a 'world turned upside down' morally and politically (Harvey 2006). The condition of the 'industrial' (or working) class had to be improved, their needs met, and society reorganized accordingly. Yet he still believed the working masses to be too ignorant and feckless to undertake this change. Moreover, he hated the violence of the French Revolution and sought peaceful change. In his opinion, society should elect industrial and economic experts to administer production and distribution. In this way, according to Saint-Simon, socialism should be brought to the masses pacifically by the State.

The second and more decisive influence on Marx and Engels was Fourier, who cynically attacked the 'civilization' (bourgeois society) of his age. He was a strong advocate of 'Harmony', believing that if humankind's natural passions were channelled effectively, a society of social cooperation would emerge. He also believed that only through voluntary cooperation could a level of production occur that would meet human needs. Property in such a society would be universalized, or made common.

Moreover, Fourier conceived of a society of communes, which he named 'phalansteries', four-storey apartment buildings in which this cooperation would take place. Workers living in the commune would choose work that interested them – about which they were passionate – and would receive in return according to their individual effort. Alongside people's material needs, their individual, sexual needs would be satisfied within the framework of the harmonious commune. Wider society, the new world order, would eventually be governed by a congress of such communes.

Marx encountered the ideas of Fourier when he was first entertaining ideas of socialism and communism at the *Rheinische Zeitung* in 1842, via Moses Hess, who frequented the socialist societies of Paris. Shortly after the Marxes arrived In Paris, Hess's émigré and journalist colleague Arnold Ruge even suggested to Marx that they should set up a Fourierist–type commune (this was never realized).

The Welsh social reformer and agitator Owen travelled to America to establish a number of self-sufficient working communities which only lasted a few years. Cabet, a popular, radical French deputy, revived the term 'communism' and gave it its modern meaning – that of a communal society. He proposed abolishing capitalism and instituting workers cooperatives; ultimately everything would be collectively owned and managed. Like Owen, Cabet set up communes in America that were similarly short lived.

It is easy to see how the ideas of these early socialists affected Marx and Engels, in their conceptions of how an ideal egalitarian society might look. Engels praised the ideas of Fourier in 1843 seeing in his 'passions' the principle of free, unforced labour (the worker willingly contributing) which would be a necessary component of a future socialist society. However, Marx denoted these thinkers as utopian (first in 1843 and later in *The Communist Manifesto*) because, although they envisioned cooperative societies, they did not explain how these societies could be attained other than as a result of the mass of people voluntarily accepting their construction.

As the authors stated in their *Manifesto*: 'The proletariat, as yet in its infancy, offers to them [utopian socialists] the spectacle of a class without any historical initiative or any independent political movement' (Marx & Engels 1848).

Marx and Engels came to see Fourierism as an important precursor to socialism/communism. In *The German Ideology* (1846) they reflected much of Fourier's vision on the reorganization of labour and satisfaction of individual passions. But they did not drop their critique of utopian socialism, holding their vision of 'scientific' socialism to be superior. In *The Communist Manifesto* they criticized the idea that workers would be the passive recipients of socialist ideas and action imparted by an enlightened minority. Instead socialism could only be achieved through a political, indeed revolutionary struggle by the working class.

The Proletariat

Marx's turn to the 'proletariat' (working class) also came about because of the face-to-face encounters with both French and (émigré) German workers in the secret socialist and communist societies of

Paris. He was deeply impressed by their revolutionary ardour. The Silesian workers strike of June 1844 instilled in Marx the idea that socialism might come about through the action from below by the industrial proletariat. Here was living proof – the first notable case of German workers engaged in prolonged collective action – that workers could struggle independently and in the face of vicious repression by the State.

Fig. 5 Friedrich Engels, 1879

Marx was deeply impressed by Engels' *Condition of the Working Class in England* (1845), which he read shortly after first meeting his future collaborator in Paris in 1844. Britain was the leading nation of the Industrial Revolution, in its 'juvenile state of capitalist exploitation' (Engels 1845). In 1842, at the age of 22, Engels had been sent by his family to Manchester, England, to work in a textile mill (and rid him of the radical sentiments so disapproved of by his father). Buying himself spare time by 'giving up the dinner-parties…of the middle classes' the young Engels spent many hours each week talking to workers. When the book was published, it laid bare the reality of rampant capitalism that he found in Manchester: poverty, soaring child and adult mortality rates, a lack of sanitation, spread of diseases, and immiseration (economic impoverishment).

Engels found these conditions to be rampant in workers' lives in and around the urban industrial centres of northwest England such as Manchester. But he denoted this situation as the 'universal' (international) condition of the proletariat in industrializing cities. In his condemnation of the system, Engels pointed to the radical political solutions of 'French and German working-class Communism [....] Fourierism and English Socialism, as well as the Communism of the German educated bourgeoisie...' (Engels 1845).

Prior to his life in Paris, Marx had believed in gradually persuading the masses of the need for socialism. Soon after arriving in Paris, however, he began to consider how socialism could be achieved through concrete political action. This coincided with his writing of the *Economic and Political Manuscripts of 1844*, in which he explained poverty and alienation (of humans) as a consequence of the division of labour and private property: the capitalist system of production.

Liberal Economics

It was an intensely productive period for Marx. Having touched on economics in his work on the State, bourgeois interests and workers conditions, he now threw himself into the study of capitalism. For this he turned to the Scottish economist Adam Smith and the English economist David Ricardo. Smith was the classical theorist of British liberal or 'laissez faire' capitalism and author of *The Wealth of Nations* (1776). He championed the free market, seeing capitalism as a natural system in which individuals' pursuit of their private interests brought about balance in society and the economy. Smith believed that left alone (by the State), the supply and demand that were inherent to such an economy would reach an equilibrium in which every commodity attained its natural price. This in turn provided income in the form of profit, rent and wages to the various social strata.

Marx then looked to Ricardo's revision of this classical theory of commodity value. Contrary to Smith, Ricardo opined that the value of a product depended on the amount of labour required to produce it. In turn, no natural balance was possible, because for the capitalist's profits to rise, the workers' wages had to fall, and vice versa. Wages and profits were inversely related; the classes had antagonistic economic interests. The hitherto social concept of class conflict was now brought to the heart of economics.

This, in essence, became Marx's labour theory of value, but that is not to say that Marx was converted to bourgeois economics. Whereas Ricardo saw the labour theory of value as a way to explain

Fig. 6 Luddites smashing textile looms which were causing falling wages and unemployment.

prices, Marx saw it as the key to understanding exploitation and inequality at the heart of the capitalist system.

Smith and Ricardo developed their theories of value in the early phase of British industrial capitalism, a time of strong tensions between all the major classes: landed aristocracy, bourgeoisie and working class. Workers' opposition to their capitalist employers was embodied by the 18th- and 19th-century 'Luddite' textile workers, who took to smashing factory machinery which they saw as threatening their livelihoods. At the same time, workers and manufacturers were brought together in a movement to repeal the 19th-century Corn Laws. These were introduced to keep grain import prices high, so as to protect the profits of Britain's own producers – the landowners. The Laws adversely affected both workers and capitalists (bourgeoisie): the former through an increase in food prices, the latter by hampering production and free trade. This led the capitalists to push down wages and thereby increase their own profits.

The bourgeois advocates of repeal (who included Ricardo) appealed to workers for support, as Marx wryly noted: 'They had entered upon the contest for the repeal of the Corn Laws, and needed the workers to help them to victory. They promised therefore, not only a double-sized loaf of bread, but the enactment of the Ten Hours' Bill' (Marx 1867). This bill, formally entitled the Factories Act 1847, limited the number of hours that women and young people (aged 13–18) were allowed to work in textile mills to ten hours per day.

Ultimately the Corn Laws were withdrawn in 1846. The movement was a major step in the emergence of the industrial capitalist from the shadow of feudalism. With aristocratic privilege undermined, the bourgeoisie gained the upper hand politically and economically, and the class struggle between bourgeoisie and proletariat took centre stage.

Although Ricardo had discovered the capital–labour antagonism at the heart of the system, still he believed, like Smith and every other mainstream economist, that capitalism was natural, and represented the highest stage of economic development. Marx, however, profoundly disagreed. In the development of his materialist conception of history, he had inverted Hegel's dialectical method of social change, to establish that bourgeois society, or capitalism, was not the be-all-and-end-all of historical progress; it had to give way to another, yet more advanced system. Such is the nature of the thesis–antithesis–synthesis evolution of ideas and paradigms. Marx would now build on the foundations of bourgeois economics to identify the contradictions within capitalism, and how these would contribute to its own downfall.

Revolution

With the onset of revolution in 1848, the working classes of France and Germany, in alliance with the liberal bourgeoisie, took on the old feudal monarchies. The French king Louis Philippe fell in February, to be replaced by a government of the Second Republic. But when the workers rose against the new regime in June, they were brutally crushed. Marx noted the merciless 'civil war' which had now been engaged between labour and capital (Marx 1848). Correspondingly, the bourgeoisie in Germany preferred to reach a settlement with the old order rather than accede to the demands of revolutionary workers.

The 1848 revolutions demonstrated to Marx that the interests of bourgeoisie and proletariat had now become diametrically opposed, and that for the workers to achieve their interests they would have to act independently and against the bourgeoisie. He concluded, moreover, that there would need to be a 'dictatorship of the proletariat' over the bourgeoisie and the rest of society, to bring about the transition to a communist society.

The revolution of 1871 – that of Parisian workers and soldiers – confirmed the powerful independence of working-class action. But the form of government that ensued, the Paris Commune, was not a true, complete form of workers' power. Although it contained important elements of a new socialist democracy, the Commune reflected the structure of a bourgeois democratic government. Moreover it excluded women, who had been central to the revolt. These weaknesses only served to confirm for Marx that the old state could not simply be taken over and used for the purposes of the workers, but had to be 'smashed' and replaced by an authentic workers' state.

Later Influences: Darwin

During the long years spent in London, Marx and Engels continued to draw inspiration from the philosophical theories and scientific discoveries of their day. Probably the single most important was the theory of evolution proposed by the English naturalist Charles Darwin in 1859. Darwin (1809–1882) argued that all life species descended from common ancestors through a process of natural selection. After reading Darwin's *On the Origin of Species* (1859), Marx declared to Engels that the theory of evolution formed the 'natural history basis of our view', in other words, of historical materialism. There were profound parallels between the ways in which both life species and human societies were born, existed and disappeared through history. In 1883, at Marx's funeral, Engels asserted that 'Just as Darwin discovered the law of development of organic nature, so Marx discovered the law of development of human history.' (Angus 2009)

3. History as the Story of Class Warfare

Karl Marx and Friedrich Engels began their world changing *The Communist Manifesto* with the following statement: 'The history of all hitherto existing society is the history of class struggle' (Marx & Engels 1848). This was a revolutionary statement; a call to arms for socialists.

The *Manifesto* represented a crystallization of the radical ideas Marx had been developing for several years. It rejected conventional views of history as either a succession of acts by or achievements of 'great men', or as a course of accidents or chance happenings. The publication of the *Manifesto* also marked the onset of a democratic revolution that swept across Europe. The startling effects of its publication ensured that it would become one of the most influential political documents of all time.

The concept of revolutionary class struggle was central to the *Manifesto*. The idea that society was divided into classes with different interests was in itself nothing new. Saint-Simon, for example, believed that for society to function effectively the needs of the working class had to be met. Furthermore, conflict between classes had been obvious to many, particularly since the

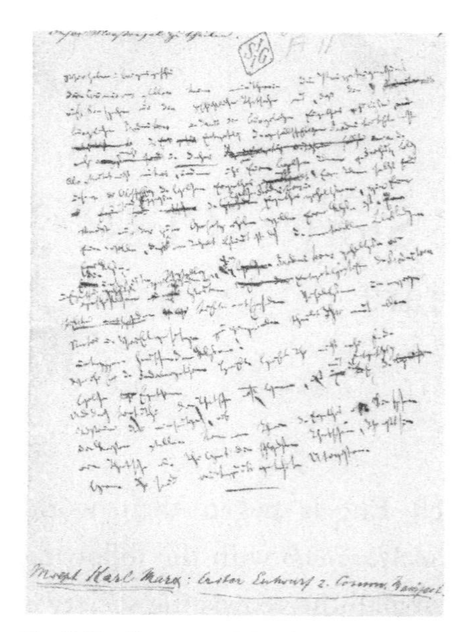

Fig. 7 The Communist Manifesto, 1847.

Great French Revolution of 1789, which had overthrown the monarchy and employed the guillotine to dispense with aristocrats and the idea that anyone had a 'divine right' to rule.

What Marx brought to the table was an understanding that the new society of industrial capitalism – essentially centred in Western Europe – was dividing into 'two increasingly hostile camps', the bourgeoisie, or capitalist class, and the proletariat, or working class. In addition, that their conflict was heading towards the overthrow of the bourgeoisie by the proletariat; and that the new state established by the proletariat would lead to the abolition of classes and the end of class society, in other words, communism (Marx 1852).

For Marx and Engels, the antagonism between classes in any given period, and in any given country, was the central driver of social change. They took as their model the countries of Europe, seeing in them the fastest developing societies. This was partly because capitalism, the most dynamic socioeconomic system that had yet existed, was born in Europe. The Industrial Revolution began in Great Britain and spread to Europe and the USA in the late 18th and early 19th centuries. By 1870, the Japanese began their own Industrial Revolution in a bid to catch up with the West.

Marx and Engels' relative lack of knowledge of non-Western countries such as India and China, and the domination of many of those places by European colonialism, led them to believe, at least initially, that these societies would have to wait for European capitalism to be overthrown by its own proletariat, in order to freely develop themselves.

Primitive Communism

Class society had not always existed. To begin with, humans lived in small egalitarian groups, the hunter-gatherer tribes that Marx and Engels later described as 'primitive communism'. This was a classless society. In such groups, everyone was involved in collecting food and would share in the fruits of their endeavours. What was produced was quickly consumed; there was no surplus. And if property existed it was communal.

But the growth of herding and agriculture from about 10,000 BCE led to the creation of an excess in production, a surplus that was appropriated by a minority of the human group. This became their private property, and in order to protect their newfound privilege they devised methods of control, both to protect their property and to compel those without to continue to produce. Human society gradually became divided into classes; essentially a divide between those who owned and controlled the means of production, and disposed of the surplus in production as they saw fit, and those who did the actual work, the direct producers.

There are various notions of social class. One conventional view sees classes as a natural part of a functional society – people divided into a hierarchy of categories in which they are conferred a certain status that may be based on income. As they work harder they may accrue wealth and gain access to a higher class. Another sociological view sees classes as various distinct groups of people having antagonistic interests, including capitalists and workers, but others too. This view says that society is just one vast marketplace in which many groups compete both with each other and within themselves for resources and status.

Marx's view was that classes are defined by their position within the system of production, the degree of ownership and control they had over the means of production, and their relationship to other classes. In the Marxist schema class is fundamentally a hierarchical and exploitative relation, with one class growing rich from the labour of another. For Marx, the ruling class in any given period is the class that owns and controls the means of production and subsistence, or the greatest share of it. This dominant class employs a large labouring class to produce a surplus which it appropriates for itself. In return the direct producer (for instance the worker) receives the means to subsist. In today's world, Mark Zuckerberg of Facebook and Jeff Bezos of Amazon are examples of members of the dominant class.

Different Historical Epochs

Each stage of society, or historical epoch, was characterized, as Marx and Engels wrote in their *Manifesto*, by the 'now hidden, now open, fight' between socioeconomic classes (Marx & Engels 1848). By this they meant that revolts and revolutions were the periodic outward expression of a permanent inner tension in any given society. This fight, they argued, 'ended either in a revolutionary reconstitution of society at large or in the common ruin of the contending classes'.

Through this lens of understanding, ancient society could be seen as divided between slave-owners and slaves, feudal society between landowners and peasants, and capitalist society between the bourgeoisie and working class.

For instance, ancient Roman society relied on the labour (both physical and mental) of slaves, the majority of whom worked in mines, mills and farms. The 'open tension' between classes was exemplified by the three 'Servile wars', when armies of slaves rose against their masters as a result of their appalling work and living conditions. Despite being roundly crushed, the slave rebellions served as inspiration to future generation of revolutionaries. Marx described Spartacus, the leader of the third Servile rebellion as:

> '*... the most splendid fellow in the whole of ancient history. Great general [...] noble character, real representative of the ancient proletariat.*'(Woods 2009)

Feudalism, which rose on the ruins of the Roman Empire and slave society in Europe and lasted around 800 years, was classically divided between lords and peasants. The late era of feudalism was marked by peasant rebellion: the French Jacquerie of 1358 when peasants rose against the nobility over high taxation and duties, and the English Peasants' Revolt of 1381 against feudal taxation and serfdom.

More importantly, 16th century Europe saw the emergence of an urban manufacturing and merchant class demanding political power, which was subsequently driven into conflict with the monarchy and nobility. In this way the revolutions in the Netherlands (1568–1648), England (1640–60) and France (1789–99) were manifestations of bourgeois revolt against the

Fig. 8 A caricature by Ferdinand Schroder on the defeat of the revolutions of 1848/49 in Europe

feudal aristocracy. Marx explains how a revolution in one country, in one era, can serve as the model for later generations, writing in December 1848:

> *'The model for the revolution of 1789 was (at least in Europe) only the [English] revolution of 1648; that for the revolution of 1648 only the revolt of the Netherlands against Spain [1566].'* (Marx 1848)

The Great French Revolution and the European revolutions of the 18th century swept away the vestiges of feudalism, by taking power away from the monarchy and aristocracy, and in turn creating the social and political conditions for capitalism to grow unchallenged – which led to the bourgeoisie becoming the ruling class. But there was an unexpected consequence: with the expansion of capitalism came also the growth of the working class.

The 1848 revolutions were emblematic not just of the struggle between aristocracy and bourgeoisie, but of that between bourgeoisie and proletariat. From this point onwards, the fundamental class tension, or struggle, within capitalist society, would be between bourgeoisie and proletariat. As Marx and Engels wrote in the *Manifesto*:

> *'Of all the classes that stand face to face with the bourgeoisie today, the proletariat alone is a really revolutionary class. The other classes decay and finally disappear in the face of modern industry; the proletariat is its special and essential product.'* (Marx & Engels, 1848)

The working class is the 'product' of capitalism, because capitalism needs labouring people to exploit – so as long as there are capitalists, or 'the bourgeoisie', there will be a working class providing the necessary labour. And these two classes will both exist together and be in eternal conflict. In fact the world has witnessed workers' uprisings, if not revolutions, against capitalist rule in many times and places: in France in 1848 and 1871, 1936 and 1968; Russia in 1905 and 1917; Germany in 1918; Spain in 1936 and many more.

Base and Superstructure

Marx and Engels analyzed and understood the phenomenon of class struggle within the framework of (or method) of historical materialism, which basically asserts that human societies and their institutions, including government and laws, arise from people's productive, economic activity.

Correspondingly, the nature of any given society in history depends on the nature of its material, or productive base. Humans live and work in societies characterized by a mode of production (the way production is organized). For instance, in the agricultural system of the feudal age, aristocrats controlled the land and exploited peasants who farmed the land, extracting from them labour, part of the harvest and tax or duties. Later, during the Industrial Revolution, production became mechanized so that machines and people worked together to produce goods in mass quantities. So both feudalism and capitalism are systems or modes of production.

Marx and Engels explained the nature of any given society using a model of 'base and superstructure', whereby the economic and technological base of the society is seen to decisively shape the political and cultural superstructure. The way people generally think and behave ultimately depends on the nature of the base; people's socioeconomic reality shapes their ideas and outlook. In capitalist societies today, individualism and productivity are prized, and capitalist populations are brought up to value money, property, possessions, appearance and fame. Whereas in earlier societies, people were encouraged to value the 'common good' of the whole society, and a person's contribution to that society far outweighed the worth of any individual accomplishments. According to Marx and Engels:

> *'The mode of production of material life conditions the social, intellectual life process in general. It is not the consciousness of men that determines their being, but, on the contrary, their social being that determines their consciousness.'* (Callinicos 2010)

In Marx and Engel's model, the base is made up of the 'forces' and 'relations' of production. The forces of production are the tools, machinery and labour required to make things. The relations are those social relationships entered into around the productive process, for example in the case of capitalism, the interrelations between boss, worker and means of production.

Together the forces and relations of production form the economic base for the (super)structure of a society which itself includes the state (government, judiciary, police, army), institutions such as the education system, culture (literature, arts and crafts) and ideology (a set of doctrines or ideas); in other words, forces that exist to justify and defend the conditions of production. As countries moved from feudalism to capitalism, the state in each case was able to gain wealth it needed to maintain its bureaucracy and army through tapping into taxes, customs, duties and state loans thrown up by a capitalist economy. In return, the state conquered countries and turned them into colonies, giving its capitalists control over world markets, and engineered laws to lessen the threat from foreign competition.

Today, a central ideological feature of modern Western capitalism is 'neo-liberalism', a policy promoted by right-wing ideologues and governments that advocates free trade, privatization and deregulation to boost firms' competitiveness and profitability. All the mechanisms of state and its institutions defend this ruling ideology as the right (or the implied 'common sense') one.

The overall complexion of the society reflects the technological stage of the productive process. Marx simplified it like this: 'the windmill gives us society with the feudal lord, the steam mill the society with the industrial capitalist' (Marx 1847). The model seems deterministic, but Engels insisted that it was a dynamic, interactive relationship:

> *'The economic situation is the basis, but the various elements of the superstructure... also exercise their influence upon the course of the historical struggles and in many cases preponderate in determining their form.'* (Engels 1890)

Just as the base–superstructure model provides us with the Marxist understanding of how society functions, so the dynamics within the model – the interaction between its various elements – gives us an understanding of how society inevitably and fundamentally changes.

The logic follows that of the dialectic from quantitative to qualitative change. In *The German Ideology*, Marx argued that changes in the forces of production lead to small cumulative changes in the relations between people which, eventually, shake up the whole organization of society. This social change occurs in the form of historical crises when contradictions develop in the base–superstructure model. Essentially, as the forces of production develop and change, the very social relations they once gave rise to eventually impede their development. This is the fundamental contradiction exposed in Marx's materialist conception of history.

From Slavery to Capitalism

The Roman Empire – in its growth and downfall – exemplifies this type of social change. The ancient Roman civilization in the Mediterranean area rested on the surplus created by slave labour. Rather than invest in and generate new techniques of production, Rome simply relied on warfare (and gathering prisoners) to increase its supply of slaves. It was an inherently inefficient economy. Then, through a combination of political, military and demographic crises, the supply of slave labour fell in the 2nd century. The economy stagnated and the slave society of ancient Rome went into decline until barbarian invasion brought it to an end.

As the Empire collapsed, landholders who had relied on its centralized, export-based economy for the sale of their products (including wine and olive oil), tried to find ways to make their estates self-sustaining. The workforce gradually shifted from slavery to serfdom, an arrangement in which unfree labourers were tied to the land. Serfs were not slaves who were treated like animals, but their rights and movements were severely restricted by the landowner. The wealth generated by their estates enabled landowners to raise armies to protect their estates from rivals and bandits.

Feudal productivity, which was essentially agricultural, took centuries to develop due to reluctance by landowners (or lords) to invest. They preferred to spend the surplus provided by the peasants to feed and arm their retainers, leaving the peasantry with little incentive to seek improved production techniques.

Feudalism gave rise to capitalism through the growth of trade and industry (represented by the bourgeoisie) in feudal societies. The towns in turn developed in a different dynamic to the rural feudal system which had given birth to them. Crucially, they drew in a pool of labour of dispossessed peasants and journeymen, the 'free' workers who would become the industrial proletariat. In contrast to the landlords, urban workshop owners used tools and crafts to increase their productivity far more quickly. By the early 14th century, areas in Flanders, Belgium and Northern Italy had acquired an urban textile economy that averaged 500 workers per atelier (workshop) – an embryonic capitalist production.

But the old feudal structures acted as a barrier to the development of capitalism, until such time as they could no longer hold back its dynamism, and open, life-or-death class struggle broke out. The English Civil War and French Revolution were examples of the way in which the growing urban middle class in each country broke the power of the monarchy and landed aristocracy to clear the path for capitalism. Marx explained the contradictions thus:

> *'From forms of development of the productive forces, these relations turn into their fetters. Then begins an era of social revolution. The changes in the economic foundation lead, sooner or later, to the transformation of the whole, immense, superstructure.'* (Marx 1859)

Capitalism in turn created the industrial working class. Compared to the slave and peasant in preceding societies, the worker was free. The slave was of course owned by the master, while the peasant had obligations to the lord. While capitalist workers were free, they had no property or independent access to the means of production, so they were forced to sell their labour power to the capitalist in order to survive.

Capital and labour are inseparable; the workers need the boss to employ them in order to make a living, but equally capitalists take on workers for their labour – it is the worker's labour, added to the materials, that constitutes the source of profit on which the capitalist's business depends. It is a relationship of exploitation, as the worker receives only a fraction of the value of what they create in the form of wages.

Inequality and Strikes

The productive forces unleashed by capitalism have created, for the first time in human history, the potential for abundance. This would be the precondition for a socialist society to exist, a society in which everyone's material needs can be met. The productive and technological advances under capitalism mean that, for instance, the working week can be reduced or the retirement age lowered. Paradoxically the opposite can, and does happen. The social relations – in other words private corporate ownership – of the means of production, prioritize increased production over reduction in labour time. Capitalism's relentless search for increasing profit, its 'need' to drive up the exploitation of workers, works against the potential improvements in people's lives. Indeed, capitalism has created a vast chasm of social inequality, standing in the way of the social transformation that Marx and Engels claimed was not only desirable, but necessary.

Although it is immensely productive, the capitalist system is inherently unstable and anarchic, creating periods of boom and slump, provoking crises of mass unemployment, poverty, famine and war around the globe. The system creates immense want and suffering alongside the potential for plenty and peace. These contradictions, stated Marx, generate resistance to the system, in the form of protest, revolt and, periodically, revolution.

According to Marx, only the working class can be the true agent of revolutionary social change, for several reasons. First, workers are forced to organize collectively. The very nature of the labour process means they must cooperate in order to produce goods and services. As a result they share a common interest in improving working conditions or obtaining higher wages. Workers join trade unions which seek to defend their interests, ultimately 'stopping competition among the workers, so that they can carry on general competition with the capitalist' (Marx 1847). It is this collective organization that gives the working class power.

Workers are uniquely placed at the heart of the labour process to disrupt production and stem the flow of profits. When a strike brings production to a halt, the company's leadership team is compelled to consider and sometimes concede to workers' demands. Mass strikes link workers from different workplaces together, enabling them to assert their interests as a class and challenge the system as a whole. For example, in the French general strike of May and June 1968, workers occupied their factories to protest against poor conditions and low wages. For the best part of two months the country was paralyzed. The president, Charles de Gaulle, eventually managed to restore order, but the government was forced to make significant concessions to the workforce.

British coal miners went on strike for over a year during 1984–85 against pit closures planned by the Conservative government of Margaret Thatcher. It was an epic strike which saw pit occupations, picket line clashes and the militancy of miners' wives. But the miners were left to fight alone and the strike eventually collapsed. This was a defeat that had far-reaching consequences for the British working class.

In 2018, the USA experienced the largest number of work days lost through strikes and stoppages since the 1980s. In an economic climate of rising profits and tax breaks for the rich, teachers, refuse collectors and hotel chain workers across the country went on strike over low pay and underfunded services, wringing significant wage rises from their employers.

Strikes happen because, although workers may accept the capitalist system as the 'natural' state of affairs, they also want built-in guarantees against its excesses. Marx wrote that workers in his time demanded a 10-hour day because the capitalists' 'demand for surplus labour appears in the drive for an unlimited extension of the working day' (Allen 2011). Similarly, one of the demands of French workers in 1968 was for the enforcement of the legal 40-hour working week (against the real average of 45–46 hours).

Other classes, such as the *petit* (small) bourgeoisie – small business owners, shopkeepers and so on – may engage in social struggles to assert their interests, but lack the necessary economic power to fundamentally change society. They can neither replace big business nor do they offer a new model of production or organization of society.

Workers and Power

Marx argued that the proletariat has a collective interest in revolutionizing society, placing the means of production under the ownership and control of those who produce. Then can begin the process of rational planning to meet social need, replacing the anarchy of market capitalism.

For this to happen, workers must contend with the power of the old ruling class. It means confronting the power of the capitalist state, part of the 'superstructure' of class society. Stemming from the antagonism between capitalists and workers, the state rises above society in order to regulate that society in the interests of the ruling class. For the most part the bourgeoisie is able to rule through persuasion, the ideology of the superstructure that tells us that the capitalist order is the natural order. However, in times of social crisis, when the antagonisms break out into open expressions of conflict – strikes, uprisings and revolutions – the bourgeoisie resorts to the organs of state power (army, police, courts, prisons) to restore its rule. With revolution comes counter-revolution.

Therefore, only when counter-revolution is defeated, and a revolutionary workers movement breaks up the capitalist state, can the necessary transition to socialism be enabled. Crucially, the means of production, previously the private property of the capitalist, would then become social property, and production would be reorganized under workers' control. The whole process involves a radical transformation of workers' ideas, Marx and Engels argued:

> *'Both for the production on a mass scale of this communist consciousness, and for the success of the cause itself, the alteration of men on a mass scale is necessary, an alteration which can only take place in a practical movement, a revolution; this revolution is necessary, therefore, not only because the ruling class cannot be overthrown in any other way, but also because the class*

> *overthrowing it can only in a revolution succeed in ridding itself of all the muck of ages and become fitted to found society anew.'* (Marx & Engels 1845)

In dialectical terms, capitalism would thus be negated by its opposite, labour, to make way for a more advanced society, socialism: a society run by the direct producers for human need. This, for Marx, would result in the disappearance of class distinctions and ultimately the 'abolition of class society' (Marx 1852).

4. Capitalism and Crisis

Marx and Engels declared capitalism to be the most advanced dynamic system the world had ever seen. It had evolved from its early agrarian and mercantile form in the early Renaissance, whereby merchant houses built their fortunes trading goods or commodities (from small scale production) between markets. Simple commodity production and exchange has a long history. As Marx wrote in *Capital*:

> *'The circulation of commodities is the starting point of capital. The production of commodities, their circulation, and that more developed form of circulation called commerce, these form the historical ground work from which it [capitalism] arises. The modern history of capital dates from the creation in the 16th century of a world-embracing commerce and a world-embracing market.'* (Marx 1867)

By the 19th century, capitalism was undergoing an industrial revolution based on factory production. In Marx's time this industrial capitalism was centred on Europe and North America, with its beginnings in China and Japan (based on the silk and porcelain industries) from the mid 1800s.

It was a system that did not recognize national boundaries. Marx and Engels wrote of the global drive of the bourgeoisie in the *Manifesto*:

> *'The need of a constantly expanding market for its products chases the bourgeoisie over the entire surface of the globe… The bourgeoisie has through its exploitation of the world market given a cosmopolitan character to production and consumption in every country.'* (Marx & Engels 1848)

Capitalism has now become a global system, witnessing exponential growth since the mid-19th century. Across the world peasants have been sucked off the land, becoming workers in the industrial zones of the new cities. With the proliferation of nation states, the working classes have grown, and the world now reflects the predominant division between bosses and workers.

In its expansion and innovation, capitalism has demonstrated the capacity of human society to produce enough for all. But by the same token it has subordinated the mass of people to the relentless pursuit of profit. The ruling capitalist class, owners of the means of production, have grown fantastically wealthy off the backs of the toiling majority, the working class. Far from meeting social need, the system has rendered miserable the lives of millions.

Capitalism has become more complex as it has conquered the world. The authors of the *Manifesto* noted the bourgeoisie's 'constant revolutionizing of the instruments of production'. Take, for example, the train. It has evolved in terms of speed and power from the steam engine of Marx's time to the twin-section diesel

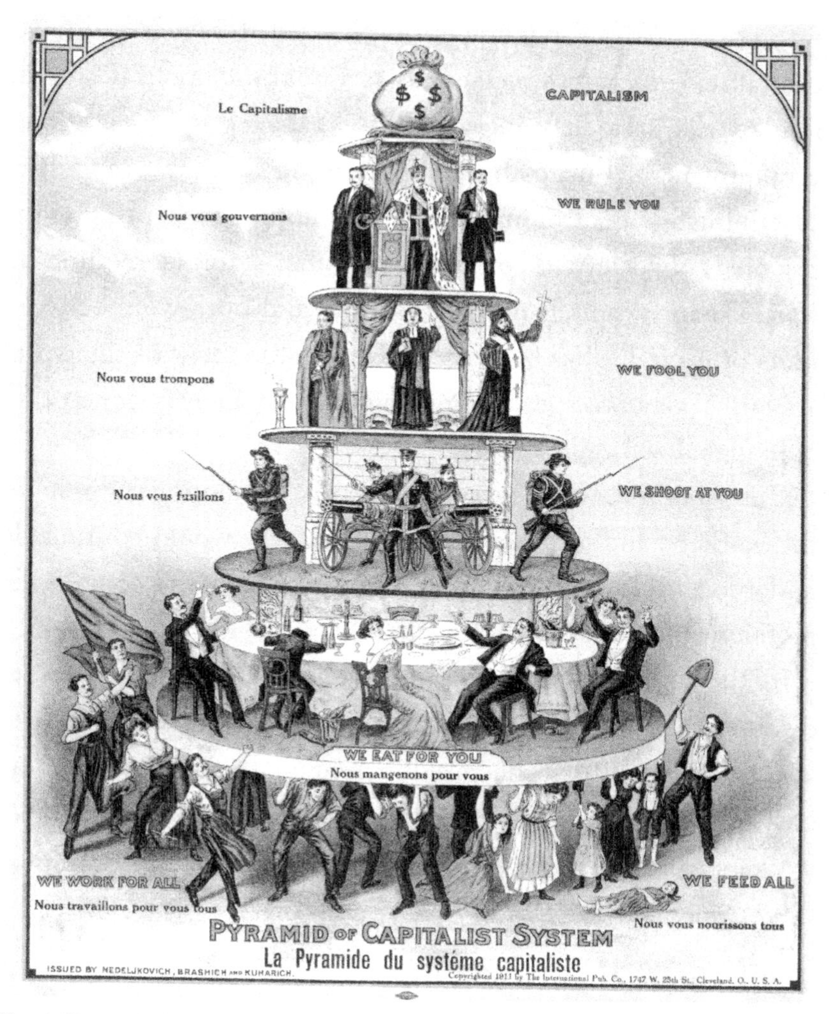

Fig. 9 'Pyramid of Capitalist System', Industrial Workers of the World (IWW) poster printed in 1911.

engine, to the high-speed train of today, in order to meet the transport needs of a rapidly developing and increasingly complex industrialized society.

The capitalist system has enjoyed periods of growth and prosperity, followed by terrible crises that have plunged society into poverty and war. Competition has led to bigger and fewer capitalists – as a system it tends towards monopolization. The role of the state has increased: as 'manager' of the national economy, regulating competition between domestic capitalists, sustaining and controlling flows of labour, and concentrating the resources of society to compete with other states (sometimes in war). Finance capitalism – the lending and borrowing between units of capital – has become a crucial component of the world system. Today, we speak of 'globalization', which is none other than globalized capitalism.

The *Manifesto* highlighted both the revolutionary role of the workers, and also how bourgeois society would continually undergo a cycle of crises generated by its inability to contain the productive forces at its disposal.

In the years that followed its publication, Marx set out to discover the inner workings of capitalism, which would in turn lead him to identify its deepest inherent contradictions, the roots of the crises that would shake the power of the bosses and impel workers to revolt. The upshot was his masterpiece of economic theory and analysis, *Das Kapital* (Capital).

The Labour Theory of Value

Marx's line of thought began by investigating the relationship of labour to commodities. The production of commodities is central to capitalism. Typically, commodities ('goods' or things, such as items of clothing or furniture) are produced for 'the market' (the people who want to buy them). Marx maintained that each commodity had a dual value: a use value and an exchange value.

The use value of a commodity relates to its usefulness to humans, in that it exists to meet human need in some way. For example, a bottle is produced in order to hold water from which we drink. The exchange value of a commodity allows for it to be swapped with another commodity (in the form of money). So a labourer might exchange the chair he made for money with which to buy clothes for his children. Marx used the formula C-M-C (Commodity-Money-Commodity) to convey this process.

Under capitalism, commodities are produced primarily for exchange, rather than for their use value. This leads to a number of key developments. First, labour itself is turned into a commodity. As the economy expands, additional labour is needed so workers are hired; they are then fired when firms hit hard times or go bust – there is no longer a need for production of goods. Labour is considered a unit cost, so the cost of the labour involved in the production of a good is factored into the total cost of its production. From the capitalist's point of view, the workforce should be flexible, bending to the needs of business, so it can be bought or not depending on market demand. From the worker's point of view, this makes for an insecure employment and income arrangement.

Second, commodity production modifies how labour is organized. In previous societies, the lord, master or chief determined work roles, but a carpenter, for instance, would own his tools and undertake the making of a complete piece of furniture or building. Under capitalism, the boss decides the division of labour, and from the earliest days of capitalism it became clear that more money could be made by breaking down the production of an item into single roles for each worker. The worker might therefore simply hit nails into hundreds of pieces of wood on a production line under this arrangement, rather than be responsible for making a whole chair.

In the modern world, this division of labour can be seen as a network of interdependent relationships in the chain of production. For example, a T-shirt goes through a lengthy cooperative process of production and distribution; it may begin as cotton farmed by peasants in Benin in Western Africa, which is then converted to thread by local factory workers. The spools are packaged and transported by lorry drivers, dock and ship workers to India. There it is coloured by textile workers in a dyeing mill and sent to garment manufacturing workers in sweatshops on the Asian subcontinent before being exported to Europe or elsewhere. And here another chain of truck drivers, warehouse workers and shop staff labour to ensure that the product can finally be put in front of the consumer and purchased.

Third, money which had been simply a means of exchange between commodities, becomes something in its own right. Where the labourer might sell a commodity to exchange it for another commodity (C-M-C), the capitalist starts with money and uses the exchange of a commodity to make more money (M-C-M). As Marx notes, 'In the one case both the starting-point and the goal are commodities, in the other they are money.' (Marx 1867)

Marx explains it like this:

> *'In the circulation C-M-C, the money is in the end converted into a commodity, that serves as a use-value; it is spent once for all. In the inverted form, M-C-M,*

on the contrary, the buyer lays out money in order that, as a seller, he may recover money. By the purchase of his commodity he throws money into circulation, in order to withdraw it again by the sale of the same commodity. He lets the money go, but only with the sly intention of getting it back again. The money, therefore, is not spent, it is merely advanced.' (Marx 1867)

Take the example of a cotton merchant.

'The cotton that was bought for £100 is perhaps resold for £100 + £10 or £110... This increment or excess over the original value I call "surplus-value." The value originally advanced, therefore, not only remains intact while in circulation, but adds to itself a surplus-value or expands itself. It is this movement that converts it into capital.' (Marx 1867)

Money becomes an end in itself; this is the capitalist's relentless pursuit of profit, 'accumulation for accumulation's sake,' as Marx intoned in *Capital* (Marx 1867). By making the workers labour more intensively and/or for longer hours, a maximum of surplus value is squeezed from them; capital that is both reinvested in the cycle of production, and used to line the pockets of the capitalist themselves.

A prime example of this is the American multinational technology and retailing company Amazon. Jeff Bezos, CEO of Amazon, is the richest man in the world, worth approximately $110 billion. He makes almost $9 million an hour. By contrast, the Amazon warehouse worker in the USA makes an average of just under $14 per hour, three dollars less than the American living wage. The company drives workers to fulfil production quotas, for example warehouse pickers are expected to pick up 400 items per hour. To keep up with the hourly rates workers cannot take bathroom breaks. Workers protest that every two to three months Amazon increases the productivity rates workers must meet to keep their jobs.

But Amazon, as the largest internet company in the world (and second largest employer in the USA) is a virtual monopoly when it comes to online retailing. Although it could easily afford to boost wages and improve conditions significantly, these are seen as impeding the cold-blooded drive for profit. Amazon does not recognize unions and even trains its managers to prevent staff from organizing in a union for better pay and conditions (Sainato 2019).

Marx compares the capitalist's love of money to that of the miser:

> *'Use-values must therefore never be looked upon as the real aim of the capitalist; neither must the profit on any single transaction. The restless never-ending process of profit-making alone is what he aims at. This boundless greed after riches, this passionate chase after exchange-value is common to the capitalist and the miser; but while the miser is merely a capitalist gone mad, the capitalist is a rational miser. The never-ending augmentation of exchange-value, which the miser strives after, by seeking to save his money from circulation, is attained by the more acute capitalist, by constantly throwing it afresh into circulation.'* (Marx 1867)

Everything Can Be Commodified

Finally with respect to capitalist production, everything becomes commodified. Things are no longer produced directly to meet our needs – the need can be induced through advertising, so the products can then be sold on the market to make a profit. This applies to services too, and anything else in which people sell their labour power in order to make a living. Later theorists in the Marxist tradition expanded the concept of commodification to understand how capitalism affects every aspect of our lives. Sex and sexuality for example, have been commodified in the form of prostitution and pornography (an industry now estimated to be worth $60–100 billion per year). Cultural production is commodified; works of art are bought and sold at randomly inflated prices in auction houses; the value of a work of literature may be gauged by its ranking on the bestseller lists; a Premiership footballer is bought for an astronomical sum to add potential to the team.

Marx went on to ask what determined the value relationship between commodities. He concluded that the only common element between different commodities is human labour. The cost of a commodity is set by the amount of human labour put into making it. Machines and tools were part of the process, but they in turn had to be produced (containing past labour) and handled (by living labour). Living labour is the key to commodity value, he said; workers are the source of profit.

Crisis and Profit

Marx argued that capitalism falls into crisis because of overproduction. Capital needs to expand – capitalists seek to accumulate in order to sell and corner as large a slice of the commodity market as possible. In prosperous ('boom') times, capitalists invest as much as they can into their businesses and step up production to the highest level, with the aim of making as much money as possible. But this means that a flood of commodities hits the market – more than can or will be bought – leading to a crisis and inevitable cut-back in production levels (the 'bust' part of the boom-bust cycle). In this way the inevitable overproduction of the capitalist model has a tendency to move forever around a boom-bust cycle. The capitalist model does not conform in any way to the traditional 'supply and demand' model it replaced, or to any other that seeks to meet consumer 'need'. This was a point Marx stressed throughout his writings.

> *'Overproduction is specifically conditioned by the general law of the production of capital: to produce to the limit set by the productive forces, that is to say, to exploit the maximum amount of labour with the given amount of capital, without any consideration for the actual limits of the market or the needs backed by the ability to pay.'* (Marx 1863)

This also complements one of the notions central to Marx's 'base and superstructure' model, namely that the social relations become 'fetters' on the productive forces – as new technologies develop, the social relations (the labourer's relation to their work) continues to relate to the older technologies and past time period. In this way the social relations hinder the new technologies and their development, creating conflict, until the new technologies eventually give rise to an inevitable social revolution that overthrows the old production relations and the superstructure.

In this way developing technologies (means of production) force a conflict with the social relations attached to older technologies and cause a social revolution. We might see this today in the rise of internet firms that have famously 'disrupted' older ways of doing certain business, such as Airbnb's disruption of the travel industry, or Uber's of the taxi industry worldwide. Marx points out that the framework of capitalism cannot contain its own productive capacities. It therefore begins to collapse.

> *'In acquiring new productive forces men change their mode of production, and in changing their mode of production, their means of gaining a living, they change all their social relations. The hand mill gives you society with the feudal lord; the steam mill society with the industrial capitalist.'* (Marx 1847)

Another, long-term tendency to crisis is that of the declining rate of profit. At the heart of capitalism is the drive for profit. Over and above any fixed amount of profit they make, the capitalist seeks to establish a healthy rate of profit – in other words a growing return on their initial investment in technology, plant, machinery and labour costs – and they want to see the levels of profit increase each year. This is not possible over the long-term. However, the competition between capitalists pushes them to accumulate ever more in order to sustain their rate of profit and acquire a greater share of the market. This means they have to further invest in the technology that will give them a decisive advantage over their rivals.

The drive to increase the productivity necessary to boost profits involves the increased mechanization of production. There are numerous examples of this process. One is the robotization of car plant assembly lines. Another is the computerization of office work. Generally speaking, machines do not completely replace workers, as they still need to be manufactured and maintained by living labour. The first capitalist to use new technology will gain a competitive advantage and make an extra profit, creating pressure for all rival capitalists to introduce that same technology into their own production. As a result, the amount of machinery across the market rises compared to the number of workers. However, workers (living labour) are the source of profit. Without their creation of *surplus* value there is no profit. Therefore, as investment in machinery rises more quickly than the labour needed to sustain it, the overall/average rate of profit begins to fall.

In this situation, capitalists have no choice but to produce at a lower level of profit. This goes against the core drive of capitalism, which is to obtain ever-increasing profit. So in this situation the capitalist seeks to offset the lower level of profit engendered by increased machinery costs by intensifying the exploitation of workers in a number of ways, which Marx referred to as 'countervailing tendencies'. One way they do this is by pushing down wages (often euphemistically called 'downward adjustments' by the leadership team) thereby extracting more profit from the worker. Another way to claw back profit through the workers is to make them work harder and for longer hours, in this way squeezing additional surplus value out of them.

Crisis and Depressions

The trouble, according to Marx, is that these countervailing tendencies are not strong enough to reverse the downward pressure on the rate of profit. The tendency of the rate of profit to fall is the built-in fissure of capitalism, leading it to enter recession on a regular basis. Moreover, he argued that each new crisis would be worse than the one before. With overproduction and declining rates of profit pushing the system into crisis, some capitalist firms go to the wall, others cut back, and unemployment rises.

Typically, workers are by far the worst affected in a capitalist crisis. The Wall Street Crash of 1929, sparking the Great Depression, led to bank closures, business failures, bankruptcies, the global collapse of share values and a worldwide fall in GDP of 15 per cent. For the working classes and poor across the industrialized world it was a catastrophe. In the USA alone unemployment rose to a quarter of the workforce – some 15 million people. For those still in work, wages dropped to starvation level. Between the late 1920s and early 1930s the hourly wage fell by 25 per cent, from 59 to 44 cents.

The Depression had terrible political consequences too, with millions in despair turning to far-right movements. It took the USA and much of the world around ten years to recover from the Great Depression, by which time fascism had triumphed in Italy, Germany and several southern European states and the world was hurtling towards war.

Capitalism usually emerges from crisis through a process of cannibalism. The bigger firms buy up the factories, machinery and materials of smaller firms that have gone bust, resulting in growing profits for the survivors. A new cycle of growth begins, only for the logic of competition to drive down profit rates again.

> *'The conditions of bourgeois society are too narrow to comprise the wealth created by them. And how does the bourgeoisie get over these crises? On the one hand by*

enforced destruction of a mass of productive forces; on the other, by the conquest of new markets, and by the more thorough exploitation of the old ones. That is to say, by paving the way for more extensive and more destructive crises, and by diminishing the means whereby crises are prevented.' (Marx 1848)

Colonialism and War

Imperialism and war have provided temporary escape routes for capitalism in crisis. Imperialism is the policy of major capitalist states to extend their power and influence over other nations through colonization, military conquest, and other means, allowing domestic capitalism to find new markets abroad. The resultant exploitation of people and resources to boost the coffers of states and their multinational companies would offset the tendency of the rate of profit to fall at 'home'.

War entails another kind of 'destruction of a mass of productive forces,' literally the physical annihilation of plant, machinery, transport networks and of course human labour power. After World War II, the victors – primarily the USA – fuelled the 'economic rejuvenation' of war-devastated Western Europe through massive injections of capital, namely the Marshall Plan. And the long post-war boom (ending in the early 1970s) was sustained by state-led investment in economies; nationalization; immigration; and new technologies.

Globalization and Crisis Today

The spread of capitalism over time and across the globe, coupled with the tendency of the rate of profit to fall, has led to what

Marx called the 'concentration' and 'centralization' of capital. By this he meant, essentially, that there are fewer but much larger firms. These large firms have swallowed up the smaller ones (centralization) and now dispose of massive amounts of capital (concentration). In today's world, some firms have grown so large that their revenue outstrips that of entire countries. The American retail chain Walmart, for instance, is bigger than Belgium in economic terms. And Coca Cola takes in more than Bolivia's GDP. If Coca Cola was a country it would rank 95th richest in the world. Small numbers of powerful multinationals wield enormous influence over our lives.

This expansion of capitalism has also involved the growth of credit and speculation. The credit system – banks and finance – emerged to facilitate the growth of businesses through borrowing and lending, creating a pool of finance that is, as Marx referred to it, 'the common capital of the ruling class' (Allen 2011).

Modern capitalism is ever more dependent on this financial system. In 2008–09, a crisis in the US subprime mortgage market led to a full-blown crisis in the international banking system. The massive government bailouts (using taxpayers' money) of banks around the world failed to prevent a knock-on recession in the USA and Europe. Millions of people in the USA lost their jobs, and the government slashed public spending. European governments also embarked on austerity programmes, cutting public spending to repay the debts incurred from saving the banks.

Some weaker European economies such as Greece, Spain, Portugal and Ireland were particularly hard hit (in the 'Eurozone crisis'). Struggling to bail out their banks or refinance their government debt, they turned to loans from powerful international institutions such as the International Monetary Fund and European Central Bank, who demanded in return even harsher austerity programmes.

Greece has been devastated by the debt crisis: it suffered a massive economic downturn in the years after 2008. In the following ten years, there were vast spending cuts accompanied by huge tax increases. Unemployment reached 28 per cent in 2013–14. According to the Organization for Economic Cooperation and Development, around a third of the population of 10 million languished in poverty in 2018; household income had fallen by 30% and people were unable to pay the bills. Even Britain, the fifth or sixth largest economy in the world, was adversely affected; in 2018 close to 14 million people were living below the official poverty line.

The financial crash of 2008 and the fate of countries such as Greece demonstrate the crisis of capitalism and the ruthless measures taken to restore the system's stability. Even so, many experts argue that austerity has failed to resolve the crisis. Business news website 'Business Insider' stated in 2018 that 'fiscal tightening' (cutting public spending to balance budgets) was damaging economic growth. A 2019 report by analysts at the think tank New Economics Foundation found that government imposed austerity in Britain had cut growth by almost £100 billion between 2008 and 2018 (Woodcock 2019).

Far from the globalized capitalism of the 21st century meeting the basic economic needs of the world's peoples, it has devastated the lives of countless millions through poverty and unemployment and offered only bleak prospects for future generations. Marx's profound analysis and withering critique of the system have rarely been more pertinent. As one of Marx's biographers stated: 'He had globalization sussed 150 years ago' (Wheen 2005).

5. Communism

In their life's work of thinking and writing, Marx and Engels sought to unlock the secrets and laws of history, human society and capitalism. In practical terms, they built international, revolutionary movements oriented on the working class. By the end of the 1800s, the organization they had helped found – the (Second) International – could stage a congress of over 800 delegates representing over 20 countries. In the same period, the European working-class movement had grown to include millions of workers organized into trade unions. The 19th century had also seen a number of revolutions that shook the bastions of wealth and privilege. After the revolutions of 1848, Marx and Engels envisioned a completely different, post-capitalist society that would completely replace the ravages of the bourgeois system: communism.

The terms 'socialism' and 'communism' were not coined by Marx. 'Socialism' was a word introduced by the utopian Comte de Saint-Simon, a French philosopher and social reformer, who Engels described as having 'the breadth of view of a genius'. The word 'communism' comes from a French word, *communisme*, which stems from another French word – *commun* – meaning 'common'. It was introduced during the Revolution of 1789, by the political agitator Gracchus Babeuf (see Chapter 2), who said that the ideal of *Liberté, Égalité, Fraternité* (Liberty, Equality, Brotherhood) could only be achieved if every member of society had the same share of property and an equal amount of money. His ideas were given a new lease of life by the utopian socialists (including Charles Fourier, Robert Owen and Moses Hess), who advocated common ownership of the means of production and the abolition of class society. The concepts of socialism and communism were central to the future society that Marx and Engels envisaged, though somewhat confusingly, they often used the terms interchangeably. In fact, Marx referred to the ideology of the post-capitalist society in a number of ways over his lifetime, including socialism, communism, positive humanism, thoroughgoing naturalism, the realm of free individuality, and a free association of producers. The multiple definitions showed the difficulty of labelling such a society, but one thing was clear for Marx: communism represented a new society of human freedom.

More precisely, however, Marx considered socialism to be a 'first' or 'lower' phase of a transition to a fully communist society. Moreover, communism would be the endpoint or goal of a dynamic process of forward movement in human history. Marx took up Hegel's concept of the 'negation of the negation' and applied it to changing human society. Capitalist society overturned or negated feudal society, and communism in turn negated capitalism. Under socialism and then communism, human relations at the point of production would be transformed in such a way that the direct producers controlled the means of production.

How exactly would this society come about? In the Manifesto Marx and Engels pointed to the revolutionary role of the workers:

> *'The weapons with which the bourgeoisie felled feudalism to the ground are now turned against the bourgeoisie itself. But not only has the bourgeoisie forged the weapons that bring death to itself; it has also called into existence the men who are to wield those weapons – the modern working class – the proletarians.'* (Marx & Engels 1968)

And in *Capital*, Marx exposed capitalism's intrinsic flaws; contradictions that would periodically push the system into crisis. Some argued that capitalism would simply collapse under the weight of its own contradictions and that working people would construct a new society from the ashes of the old. But Marx and Engels never wavered in their conviction that workers needed to wage a revolutionary struggle for socialism.

To do so, the proletariat needed to move from being a 'class in itself'– a class objectively exploited and oppressed under capitalism – to a 'class for itself', in other words, conscious of its collective power and interests, opposition to the bourgeoisie, and revolutionary role.

> *'Economic conditions had first transformed the mass of the people of the country into workers. The combination of capital has created for this mass a common situation, common interests. This mass is thus already a class as against capital, but not yet for itself. In the struggle, of which we have noted only a few phases, this mass*

> *becomes united, and constitutes itself as a class for itself. The interests it defends become class interests. But the struggle of class against class is a political struggle.'* (Marx 1885)

There were powerful obstacles standing in the way of workers' unity and self-consciousness as a class. Not least the prevailing ideas in bourgeois society. How could workers rid themselves of these ideas and establish a state that reflected their own interests?

Power and the Ruling Ideas

Most of the time, the majority of working people accept capitalism, in spite of the exploitation and oppression they experience. The system does not dominate primarily through physical force – workers are not compelled to produce with a gun to their head. As individuals they are free to sell their labour power, which they do to the highest bidder, or at least to the capitalist who will hire their skills in return for a living wage. Furthermore, they compete with other workers for the job. And even though production naturally depends on cooperation between workers, workplace discipline – pressure from managers, middle managers and foremen – also compels workers to think and operate as individuals within the workplace. The capitalist's ownership and control of the means of production, and the impersonal forces of the market, appear to most of their workers as 'natural'.

It is not that workers are uneducated or are not intelligent enough to realize the unfairness of their position and the inequity of the system. Today we have highly technical and skilled workers, computer programmers, airline pilots or university teachers who understand what is required for their workplace to function. In manual factory jobs, too, the workforce – by virtue of their need to cooperate – often know how to run the workplace better than the boss.

Even if workers hate the poverty and inequality created by capitalism, and dislike their boss, landlord, or mortgage lender, most come to see these as inevitable, the way the world works and part of 'human nature'. Capitalist society is considered the natural state of affairs, or at least there is no alternative. This is because, as Marx argued in 1846:

> *'The ideas of the ruling class are in every epoch the ruling ideas, i.e. the class which is the ruling material force of society, is at the same time its ruling intellectual force. The class which has the means of material production at its disposal has control at the same time over the means of mental production, so that thereby, generally speaking, the ideas of those who lack the means of mental production are subject to it.'*

Whoever holds power, through holding the economic reins, also establishes the dominant ideas of any society. Therefore the main barrier to workers uniting to overthrow capitalism is the ideas in their heads, effectively 'ruling class ideology'. By 'ideology' is meant a set of ideas and values reflecting the interests of a given social grouping that aims to bind others to the aims and objectives of that group.

Today, rulers of capitalist (or bourgeois) societies claim to govern by values of freedom, democracy, and tolerance. Yet they cannot fully hide class divisions, so seek to persuade people that the rich and powerful rule because of their alleged greater intelligence, sophistication or cultural capital than the rest of us.

Dividing Ideas

The ruling class also relies on ideas of division and discrimination to maintain its rule. Perhaps the central plank of bourgeois ideology is that of nationalism, the idea that in spite of divisions of wealth and status we are bound together within 'the nation' – within distinct geographical borders, sharing a common language and part of a territorial or local community.

Yet how could, for example, German workers have the same interests as German capitalists if their socio-economic interests were diametrically opposed? While recognizing the conflict between each 'national' working class and its own rulers, Marx and Engels were internationalists who saw nationalism as a dangerous illusion. They wrote in the *Manifesto*: 'The communists are reproached with desiring to abolish countries and nationality. The working men have no country. We cannot take from them what they have not got.' (Marx & Engels 1848)

However, they distinguished between different types of nationalism, opposing the colonial subjugation of small countries by imperial nations. Apart from the violence and oppression of colonialism, nationalist ideas also bound workers to their ruling class and set them against workers of other nationalities. For example, when it came to the centuries-old question of Irish independence from British rule, Marx wrote:

> *'Every industrial and commercial centre in England now possesses a working class divided into two hostile camps, English proletarians and Irish proletarians. The ordinary English worker hates the Irish worker as a competitor who lowers his standard of life. [...] He*

> *cherishes religious, social, and national prejudices against the Irish worker. [...] This antagonism is artificially kept alive and intensified by the press, the pulpit, the comic papers, in short, by all the means at the disposal of the ruling classes. This antagonism is the secret of the impotence of the English working class, despite its organization. It is the secret by which the capitalist class maintains its power. And the latter is quite aware of this.'* (Marx 1932)

It was in reference to Irish freedom from British rule that Marx penned the famous epithet 'one nation that enslaves another forges its own chains' (which is particularly apposite today, when Ireland, formerly 'enslaved' by Britain, found itself unbreakably chained to it during Brexit negotiations. In his day Marx attacked the centre of the British Empire – England – as the 'metropolis of capital' (Marx 1985), a centre which plundered and exploited a much larger periphery, extracting the surplus value of the mass of working people in poorer nations or territories.

> *'The discovery of gold and silver in America, the extirpation, enslavement and entombment in mines of the indigenous population of that continent, the beginnings of the conquest and plunder of India, and the conversion of Africa into a preserve for the commercial hunting of black skins are all things that characterize the dawn of the era of capitalist production. These idyllic proceedings are the chief moments of primitive accumulation. In fact the veiled slavery of the wage labourers in Europe needed the unqualified slavery of*

> *the New World as its pedestal... Capital comes dripping from head to toe, from every pore, with blood and dirt.'* (Marx 1867)

Marx was clear that for workers to unite, they had to recognize and combat nationalism and racism, and the divisive myths or lies put out by their own rulers. For Marx, internationalism was synonymous with anti-imperialism.

The ideology of nationalism is bolstered by the display of symbols, including monarchy, flag, national anthem, army, navy and so on; so many institutions that bind us to our rulers. Children at school are taught the 'national' history and are encouraged to share in certain myths. A British worker may think, 'My life is hard, my family is poor... but at least I'm British, at least we have the Queen'. Marx would describe this as a form of false consciousness that masks the worker's objective interests, suggesting that in the (socialist) future, 'the supremacy of the proletariat will cause [differences between the nations] vanish still further' (Marx & Engels 1848).

We are led to distinguish ourselves from other peoples by virtue of nationality. This can take the form of chauvinism towards those of different nationalities, and from the vantage point of whites in, say, the Western world, racism towards people of Asian, African and Latin American nationality or descent. Nationalism is the ideological glue by which our rulers ask us to rally to the flag, to join the army and fight in or support a war.

Marx recognized war as an outgrowth of the political and economic competition between nations, but his individual stance on particular wars was contingent on how they enhanced (or not) the class struggle between the bourgeoisie and proletariat, particularly in the advanced capitalist nations of his day. He therefore supported the industrial North against the plantation South in the American Civil War, as it set the forces of economic progress against reaction, and free workers against slavery.

Fig. 10 Franco-Prussian War, Strasbourg, 15 October, 1870.

When it came to the Franco-Prussian War of 1870, Marx was more circumspect, given that these were two major powers with imperial ambitions. Although he appeared to favour a German victory, because he believed that it would hasten a revolution in France (partly realized by the Paris Commune), he called the national war 'a disgusting exhibition on both sides'. Moreover, he applauded the German socialists' vote against war credits (funding) in the Reichstag, and remarked that in both France and Germany, workers' opposition to the war was growing. Speaking of French workers, he noted in a letter to Paul and Laura Lafargue on 28 July 1870:

> *'At the same time they say: "The plague on both your houses"... For my own part, I do everything in my power, through the means of the International, to stimulate this "Neutrality" spirit...'*

Marx hoped that internationalism would prevail and French and German workers unite in opposition to the war, rather than slaughter each other in the name of their respective 'national interest'.

Similarly, Marx called for English workers to discard their hostility towards the Irish, and white workers in the USA to seek unity with black workers. He saw racism as a tool used by the political class and establishment to divide workers of different nationalities and ethnicities, and thereby weaken the common struggle they discover to challenge the system. As he wrote in *Capital* with reference to racism rooted in the slavery of his times: 'Labour cannot emancipate itself in the white skin where in the black it is branded.' (Marx 1870)

The prejudice and hostility towards those of different nationality or ethnicity, fostered by politicians and the media in Marx's time, find a contemporary parallel in xenophobia and anti-immigrant racism across the Western world today. Examples include US President Donald Trump's denunciation of Mexican immigrants as criminals and rapists; British Primeminister Boris Johnson lampooning veiled Muslim women as 'letterboxes'; the French authorities' denigration of Roma people, smashing up their camps and deporting them, and the list goes on.

Always and everywhere Marx encouraged his followers and workers to fight to overcome the divisions between workers. As the 1880 programme of the French Workers Party, co-authored by Marx, stated, 'the emancipation of the productive class is that of all human beings without distinction of sex or race' (Fernbach 1992).

Besides race, the reference to gender in this declaration underlined the fact that Marx also understood the subordinate role of women under capitalism, and the need to overcome their oppression. This applied to women of all classes. Indeed, Marx and Engels in the *Manifesto* attacked the bourgeois family model, held up by the ruling class as the epitome of morality and propriety.

> *'On what foundation is the present family, the bourgeois family, based? On capital, on private gain. In its completely developed form, this family exists only among the bourgeoisie. But this state of things finds its complement in the practical absence of the family among the proletarians, and in public prostitution.'* (Marx & Engels 1848)

In the mid-19th century Industrial Revolution, women and children were driven into the inhuman working conditions of the factory system, making 'family life' virtually impossible.

> *'The bourgeois clap-trap about the family and education, about the hallowed co-relation of parents and child, becomes all the more disgusting, the more, by the action of Modern Industry, all the family ties among the proletarians are torn asunder, and their children transformed into simple articles of commerce and instruments of labour.'* (Marx & Engels 1848)

Accordingly Marx and Engels pushed for the abolition of child labour and legislation to improve women's conditions. The 1880 Programme, for example, contained the economic demand of equal pay for equal work for all genders. But this was not just to better the condition of women and the working family in the short term. More importantly, they saw that workers' struggle would accelerate the downfall of capitalism and with it the prevailing family model.

And while middle class or bourgeois women led (by comparison) materially comfortable lives, Marx and Engels saw them as chained to the family and sexually subjugated to their husbands (and other men). The prevailing 'tyranny' of the family was analogous to capitalism in that it reproduced the inequality of social relations, and caused personal crises similar to revolutions, Marx noted (Marx 1846).

In his later work, *The Origin of the Family, Private Property, and the State* (1884), which drew on Marx's notebooks, Engels theorized that women's oppression was rooted in the history of class society and came to be enshrined in the institution of the family. He termed it the 'world historic defeat of the female sex'. Yet it was a defeat that could be reversed. As he and Marx argued in the *Manifesto*, 'The bourgeois family will vanish as a matter of course when its complement [working class family] vanishes, and both will vanish with the vanishing of capital.'

Although women's lives have improved considerably since Marx's time, they are still the primary carers in Western homes while earning substantially less than men at work. The Income Gender Gap report of 2018 showed that globally, a woman earns on average just over half a man's wage ($12k: $23k). Additionally, women are by far the main victims of rape and sexual violence, and the female body is especially commodified in advertising and pornography. The struggle for women's liberation goes on.

Workers' Self-emancipation

Marx further contended that fundamental change could not be carried through on behalf of the workers by a party or individuals claiming to stand for the proletariat. For Marx, socialism could not be engineered by an enlightened minority, as the early utopian socialists had believed. On the contrary, it was a battle that had to be waged 'from below', according to Marx; flesh and blood workers engaged in a revolutionary struggle to break the power of the bourgeoisie. As Marx declared in the opening line of the general rules of the First International: 'The emancipation of the working class must be conquered by the workers themselves.' (Marx 1867)

However, the process is not automatic. Although the class struggle is a permanent feature of capitalist society, it proceeds in degrees and intensity. Under 'normal' conditions under capitalism, only small numbers of workers will be on strike or in dispute with their bosses, but every few years there can be waves of strikes in different sectors of the workforce. And from time to time a general (mass) strike can draw in a majority (or large part) of workers.

Historically, trade union organization has been a sign of the combativity of workers, as these organizations have sought to wrest concessions from the employers over wages and conditions. Ultimately, workers' willingness and ability to fight depends on their levels of confidence and organisation. The British workers' movement, for instance, suffered a number of defeats in the 1980s (miners', dockers', seafarers' strikes) from which it is still recovering. Class struggle in the USA, on the other hand, has undergone a revival, with workers in teaching and retail going on the offensive in the last few years over conditions and pay. At the same time, India has witnessed the biggest general strikes in human history, with 150–180 million workers mobilized by their unions against the government's economic policies.

Furthermore the anarchic nature of capitalism and its unforeseen crises push workers into struggle in different numbers, industries and at different points in time. There is not a linear route from mass strike to socialism. Marx and Engels noted the unpredictable nature of social revolt:

> *'Men make their own history, but they do not make it as they please; they do not make it under self-selected circumstances, but under circumstances existing already, given and transmitted from the past. The tradition of all dead generations weighs like a nightmare on the brains of the living.'* (Marx 1852)

It was because of this tremendous unevenness in the experience of workers that Marx and Engels advocated political organization, including membership of groups such as the Communist League and the IWA (International Working Men's Association). The aim was to achieve a measure of independence of the proletariat from the bourgeoisie and bourgeois ideas, and help shape the struggles of workers. In *The Communist Manifesto* they spoke of the leading role of the Communists:

> *'The Communists, therefore, are, on the one hand, practically the most advanced and resolute section of the working-class parties of every country, that section which pushes forward all others; on the other hand,*

> *theoretically, they have over the great mass of the proletariat the advantage of clearly understanding the lines of march, the conditions, and the ultimate general results of the proletarian movement. The immediate aim of the Communists is the same as that of all other proletarian parties: formation of the proletariat into a class, overthrow of the bourgeois supremacy, conquest of political power by the proletariat.'* (Marx & Engels 1848)

Socialism and Communism

In his *Critique of the Gotha Programme*, Marx wrote:

> *'...between capitalist and communist society there lies the period of the revolutionary transformation of the one into the other. Corresponding to this is also a political transition period in which the state can be nothing but the revolutionary dictatorship of the proletariat.'* (Marx 1875)

The last phrase has been often misinterpreted, or misapplied so as to mean an oppressive tyranny, akin to the Stalinist regimes of the ex-Soviet Union and Eastern Bloc. What Marx actually had in mind was a transitional state that could forcibly prevent the restoration of the old order while installing the rule of a new order, that of the direct producers. Only under these conditions would class divisions begin to disappear, and the state wither away.

Marx detected the indices of this future state in the experience of the 1871 Paris Commune:

> *'The Commune was formed of the municipal councillors, chosen by universal suffrage in the various wards of the town, responsible and revocable at any time. The majority of its members were naturally working men, or acknowledged representatives of the working class.... The police, which until then had been the instrument of the Government, was at once stripped of its political attributes, and turned into the responsible, and at all times revocable, agent of the Commune. So were the officials of all other branches of the administration. From the members of the Commune downwards, the public service had to be done at workmen's wages. The privileges and the representation allowances of the high dignitaries of state disappeared along with the high dignitaries themselves.... Having once got rid of the standing army and the police, the instruments of physical force of the old government, the Commune proceeded at once to break the instrument of spiritual suppression, the power of the priests.... The judicial functionaries lost that sham independence... they were thenceforward to be elective, responsible, and revocable.' (Marx 1871)*

There were problems with this model, not least that Parisian women were excluded from voting. But the outline of a genuine workers' democracy was apparent.

History has since furnished us with several examples of revolutionary situations in which workers established their own organs of rule. In 1917, for example, the *Soviets* (workers' councils) in Russia were local, regional and national bodies of

Fig. 11 Makeshift barricades are constructed by the Paris Commune to keep out the French Army during *La Semaine Sanglante* (Bloody Week), 1871.

workers' representatives. A factory council would elect delegates to a committee that could both manage the factory and in turn send delegates to a higher council of the industry. The council fulfilled both an economic and political role. In this way the workers could take control of the process of production and goods could be manufactured and distributed according to a plan that met both the needs of these workers and those of wider society. The government would effectively rest on the network of workers' councils, thus ensuring the accountability of government and deputies to the people.

The Spanish revolutionary Andreu Nin wrote of the early Russian Soviets:

> *'Never before was there such an organization that could count on such unlimited confidence on the part of the*

> *masses and which was so closely connected with them. The workers in the factories elected their deputies to the Soviet. The latter had to provide an account of their deeds to those who elected them and it was common for those deputies who did not satisfactorily fulfil the mission delegated to them by their constituency to be dismissed and replaced by another deputy.'* (Nin 1932)

This workers' democracy of the early Soviet Union was eviscerated by civil war, economic crisis and Josef Stalin's rise to power. Even so, it proved in its brief lifespan far more democratic than bourgeois democracy, because people could regularly participate in making important decisions that directly affected their lives and the welfare of society. Representatives would be accountable and subject to recall if they did not implement the wishes of the people.

Along with the establishment of a workers' democracy, production would come under workers' control:

> *'The proletariat will use its political supremacy to wrest, by degree, all capital from the bourgeoisie, to centralize all instruments of production in the hands of the state, i.e., of the proletariat organized as the ruling class; and to increase the total productive forces as rapidly as possible.'* (Marx 1848)

This is what Marx and Engels referred to as the 'dictatorship of the proletariat'. The phrase has often been used to malign Marx and Marxism in general, with critics again pointing to the regimes of the former Eastern Bloc. However, what it actually meant for Marx was the democratic rule of the working class – the majority of the people – collectively engaged in the decision-making processes.

More broadly, Marx did not provide concrete answers to the question of how communism – the most mature stage of socialism – would look. There was no blueprint. In a letter to his philosopher friend Arnold Ruge, Marx wrote: 'We do not anticipate the world dogmatically, but rather wish to find the new world through the criticism of the old.' (Marx 1843)

Marx, Engels and some later Marxists envisioned a society that held reverse, contradictory priorities to those of capitalism. In the Manifesto, Marx and Engels further outlined a series of measures that a socialist, or workers' state would – or should – implement, which included abolition of private property, progressive income tax, nationalization of the means of production, merging of agriculture with manufacturing industries, free education, and equal liability of all to labour.

For Marx, it was not enough that there should be only common ownership of property (he termed it 'crude' communism) whereby the state nominally took control of the means of production, land and infrastructure; workers had to exercise democratic control over this public property.

These were temporary measures that a socialist state could take in the short term, establishing the groundwork for a planned economy. Marx and Engels saw the need to speed up industrialization in order to create the society of plenty that could sustain socialism, and eventually, communism. The former rulers, employers, managers would be brought to the level of workers, 'the proletariat organised as the ruling class'.

In other words, there would be a reversal of the former social relations, then a levelling out – with each person contributing to the productive process.

With the transitional period having established workers' control, and production directed to meeting human need, there would be 'the abolition of buying and selling, of the bourgeois conditions of production, and of the bourgeoisie itself' (Marx & Engels 1848). Once the direct producers had achieved ownership and control of the productive process, then the class distinctions of boss/worker and rich/poor would disappear, and frictions between white- and blue-collar workers or urban and rural workers would fade away. With class differences wiped away, the state would become obsolete.

In 1875, Marx used the following phrase to express the working principle of communism: 'From each according to their ability, to each according to their needs' (Marx 1875). People would be expected to contribute based on their skills, abilities and aptitudes in the context of a planned society. They would perform fulfilling work, receiving in return the necessities of life – food, clothing and shelter. Eventually, all could partake in the abundance that free labour could produce.

Crucially, this would end alienation, the lack of fulfilment that working people feel under capitalism. For the worker, alienation means estrangement from the fruits of their labour. By acquiring ownership and control over what is produced, they rediscover a purpose and meaning in work, their life-activity. By extension their relations with other people, too, are transformed.

Over time, technological advances would reduce or eliminate the menial, boring and repetitive tasks of working life, leading to a massive reduction in the working day, and ultimately the erasure of the division between work and leisure. In *The German Ideology*, Marx summed up the contrast between work under capitalism and communism:

> *'For as soon as the distribution of labour comes into being, each man has a particular, exclusive sphere of activity, which is forced upon him and from which he cannot escape. He is a hunter, a fisherman, a herdsman, or a critical critic, and must remain so if he does not want to lose his means of livelihood; while in communist society, where nobody has one exclusive sphere of activity but each can become accomplished in any branch he wishes, society regulates the general production and thus makes it possible for me to do one thing today and another tomorrow, to hunt in the morning, fish in the afternoon, rear cattle in the evening, criticise after dinner, just as I have a mind, without ever becoming hunter, fisherman, herdsman or critic.'* (Marx, 1845)

The reference to herdsmen and hunter pertained of course to occupations more prevalent in Marx's time. But the principle of free and diverse labour still holds.

Liberated from the drudgery and routine of the capitalist working day, and living in a cooperative society where their basic needs are met, people would be able not only to perform meaningful work but to develop their individual creative potential to the fullest. Education would be geared towards teaching people to master a wide range of skills. Consequently, science would devolve from experts to the citizenry. People could develop their physical health through sports and exercise. Marx talked of how communist society would end the specialization of painting for instance, bringing artistic endeavour to the masses.

Marx said that he sought 'to find the new world through the criticism of the old'. He viewed capitalism not purely as an economic system, but as a system of social relations, so that the alternative to capitalism – communism – would transform the whole of human society in its perspectives and interrelationships. It was a bold and revolutionary vision.

Conclusion

Sales of *Das Kapital*, Marx's masterpiece of political economy, have soared ever since 2008, as have those of *The Communist Manifesto* and Engels' *Outlines of the Critique of Political Economy.* Their sales rose as British workers bailed out the banks to keep the collapsing system going, ensuring that those profiting most from capitalism – the bankers and others in the financial sector – remained secure while other workers struggled with debt, job insecurity or worse. Interest in Marx's work rose globally to such an extent that Chinese theatre director He Nian created an all-singing, all-dancing musical based on *Das Kapital* in Beijing, with strict guidelines that Marx's theories not be distorted. (Branigan, 2012).

At that point, it had been only four years since the 2008 financial crash and politicians and 'experts' were still scratching their heads as to its causes. With the bankruptcy of the Lehman Brothers investment firm in the USA and collapse of the banking system, governments in the West decided they had no choice but to prop it up – using such vast sums of money that many countries were plunged into recession (in many cases technically more severe than that of the Wall Street Crash of 1929). No wonder Marx was making a comeback.

In fact, Marxism's influence has waxed and waned over the last 150 years. In the post-war era especially, many regarded Karl Marx's theories as archaic, and Marx himself was branded a 'despotic' revolutionary whose ideas led to totalitarianism. His writings were further besmirched following the collapse of the so-called communist regimes in Eastern Europe.

Yet in subsequent years Marx's ideas proved their resilience, seeming to make sense of a 21st century world gone mad. In the UK in 2005, a BBC radio poll named Marx as the listeners' most popular philosopher, prompting a hysterical reaction from right-wing bourgeois newspaper *The Daily Mail* that referred to the political philosopher as 'Marx the Monster'.

With the Great Recession affecting world markets during the late 2000s and early 2010s, Marx's prediction that capitalism, a system fraught with contradictions, would skewer itself, appeared to be coming true (again). Yet how could 21st century globalized capitalism, a sophisticated system with all its technological knowhow, crash and burn in this way? The flaw, as Marx suggested, lay not just with the greed of individual bankers, financiers and capitalists, but in the very essence of capitalism, whose unyielding drive for profit has laid waste to the world while sowing the seeds of its own demise.

What's more, as governments everywhere were bailing out banks and drawing up austerity programmes that would make their populations repay the debts incurred over many years, the prospect of revolt from below loomed. When in 2011 the Egyptian masses rose up against the Mubarak regime, this too seemed to vindicate Marx's belief in the revolutionary struggle for socialism as the remedy to the iniquities of capitalism.

From early on in his political career, every word Marx wrote or spoke was geared towards the transformation of the world, against the rulers, and in support of the mass of working people. He fought to end centuries of hierarchy, alienation and exploitation, to attain the realm of human freedom and equality. His ideas were about revolution, and they were revolutionary ideas. For Marx, 'philosophers had only interpreted the world. The point however, is to change it' (Marx 1845).

This made Marx a dangerous proposition for the powers that be, so much so that he became a political exile, shunted with his ailing wife and children around the capitals of Western Europe. He forsook a life of bourgeois respectability and comfort to further the cause of human liberation.

By the time Marx and Engels had published their *Communist Manifesto*, Europe was engulfed in revolution. And within 30 years the world caught its first glimpse of workers' power, in the shape of the Paris Commune in 1871, which governed Paris for two months before being brought down by the French Army. The time seemed ripe for a radical break with capitalism. But the promised proletarian, socialist revolution did not materialize – at least not for several decades after Marx and Engels' deaths. However, the 1917 Russian Revolution, and other revolutionary situations in which workers played a major role, were isolated and ultimately failed to fashion a new, global society of cooperation and freedom.

Some 150 years after the publication of *Das Kapital*, most countries still live under capitalism, and continue to endure its gross inequality and rampant oppression. By capitalist economists' own calculations, one per cent of the world's population now owns over half the world's wealth (Neate 2017). The richest man in the world earns 600,000 times more per hour than one of his workers – and he makes it from the 'surplus' gained from his workers' labour.

Food is thrown away, or crops are destroyed because production quotas are exceeded and the 'right' market price cannot be found. Yet people starve. Famine grips entire populations in Eastern Africa. At the same time, billions are being spent by governments on weapons and wars. The competition between states for power and control of resources has exacted a huge toll on the world's population, particularly in the Middle East. One study estimates the numbers of (mostly civilian) deaths in US-led or sponsored wars since 2001 at six million (Davies 2018).

Capitalism has also instigated runaway climate change and pollution. The major powers continue to subsidize fossil fuel companies while the icecaps melt. The Amazon rainforest – the 'lungs of the world' – burns to satisfy the profit margins of agribusiness, facilitated by the politicians. Scientists estimate that we are losing dozens of animal species every day as ecosystems unravel under the impact of climate change.

The challenges posed by 21st century capitalism lend renewed urgency to Marx's calls for radical change. Could a socialist revolution still happen? There is no Marxist crystal ball. We can use his dialectical methods and ideas to analyze and understand events, and give indicators as to how the future might unfold. But more fundamentally for Marx and Engels, theory cannot be divorced from practice: people need to engage in a political struggle to challenge and overturn capitalism.

In 2018 the people of Sudan, Hong Kong and Ecuador, American teachers, French 'yellow vests' and school student climate strikers everywhere erupted in anger against a political and economic order that threatens not just their livelihoods but the future of the planet. They echo Marx's central message that collectively, working people can make a difference when they choose to fight. And more so: they can transform themselves and the world.

Bibliography

Works by Marx

Marx, K. (1842) 'Debates on Law on Thefts of Wood'. *Rheinische Zeitung*. Nos. 298, 300, 303, 305 and 307.

Marx, K. (1843) Letter to Arnold Ruge. Available at https://www.marxists.org/archive/marx/works/1843/letters/43_09-alt.htm (Accessed: 5 September 2019).

Marx, K. (1845) 'Theses on Feuerbach'. Available at https://www.marxists.org/archive/marx/works/1845/theses/theses.htm (Accessed: 5 September 2019).

Marx, K. and Engels, F. (1845) *The German Ideology*. Available at https://www.marxists.org/archive/marx/works/1845/german-ideology/ch01d.htm (Accessed: 5 September 2019).

Marx, K. and Engels, F. (1845) *The German Ideology. Part I: Feuerbach. Opposition of the Materialist and Idealist Outlook*. Available at https://www.marxists.org/archive/marx/works/1845/german-ideology/ch01b.htm (Accessed: 5 September 2019).

Marx, K .and Engels, F. (1846) *Collected Works, Vol. 5 (The German Ideology)*. Available at https:// https://archive.org/details/Marx-Engles-German-Ideology (Accessed: 5 September 2019).

Marx, K. (1847) *The Poverty of Philosophy*. Available at https://www.marxists.org/archive/marx/works/1847/poverty-philosophy/ch02e.htm (Accessed: 5 September 2019).

Marx, K. and Engels, F. (1848) *The Communist Manifesto*. London: The Communist League.

Marx, K. (1848) 'The June Revolution', *Neue Rheinische Zeitung*, June. Available at https://www.marxists.org/archive/marx/works/1848/06/29a.htm (Accessed: 5 September 2019).

Marx, K. (1848) 'The Bourgeoisie and the Counter-revolution', *Neue Rheinische Zeitung*, No. 169, December. Available at https://www.marxists.org/archive/marx/works/1848/12/15.htm (Accessed: 5 September 2019).

Marx, K. (1852) 'Marx to J. Weydemeyer in New York'. 5 March. Available at https://www.marxists.org/archive/marx/works/1852/letters/52_03_5-ab.htm (Accessed: 5 September 2019).

Marx, K. (1852) Letter to J.Weydemeyer. Available at https://www.marxists.org/archive/marx/works/1852/letters/52_03_5-ab.htm (Accessed: 5 September 2019).

Marx, K. (1852) *The Eighteenth Brumaire of Louis Bonaparte (Part 1)*. Available at https://www.marxists.org/archive/marx/works/1852/18th-brumaire/ch01.htm (Accessed: 5 September 2019).

Marx, K. (1859) *A Contribution to the Critique of Political Economy*. Available at https://www.marxists.org/archive/marx/works/1859/critique-pol-economy/preface.htm (Accessed: 5 September 2019).

Marx, F. (1861) 'Letter to Engels in Manchester'. 27 February. Available at https://www.marxists.org/archive/marx/works/1861/letters/61_02_27-abs.htm (Accessed: 5 September 2019).

Marx, K. (1863/1969) *Theories of Surplus Value, Vol.2*. London: Lawrence & Wishart.

Marx, K. (1867) 'Conversion of surplus value into capital'. *Capital*. Available at https://www.marxists.org/archive/marx/works/1867-c1/ch24.htm (Accessed: 5 September 2019).

Marx, K. (1867) *Capital*. (Afterword to the Second German Edition). Available at https://www.marxists.org/archive/marx/works/1867-c1/p3.htm (Accessed: 5 September 2019).

Marx, K. (1867) Rules and Administrative Regulations of the International Workingmen's Association. Available at https://www.marxists.org/history/international/iwma/documents/1867/rules.htm (Accessed: 5 September 2019).

Marx, K. (1871) 'The Third Address'. *The Civil War in France*. Available at https://www.marxists.org/archive/marx/works/1871/civil-war-france/ch5.htm (Accessed: 5 September 2019).

Marx, K. (1875) *Critique of the Gotha Programme (Part 1)*. Available at https://www.marxists.org/archive/marx/works/1875/gotha/ch01.htm (Accessed: 5 September 2019).

Marx, K. (1875) *Critique of the Gotha Programme (Part 4)*. Available at https://www.marxists.org/archive/marx/works/1875/gotha/ch04.htm (Accessed: 5 September 2019)

Other works cited

Allen, K. (2011) *Marx and the Alternative to Capitalism*. London: Pluto.

Angus, I. (2009) 'Marx and Engels… and Darwin?', *International Socialist Review*, No. 65. Available at https://isreview.org/issue/65/marx-and-engelsand-darwin (Accessed: 5 September 2019).

Branigan, T. (2009) 'China to bring Das Kapital to life on Beijing stage', *The Guardian*, 17 March. Available at https://www.theguardian.com/world/2009/mar/17/china-das-kapital-marx-stage (Accessed: 5 September 2019).

Callinicos, A. (2010) T*he Revolutionary Ideas of Karl Marx*. London: Bookmarks.

Davies, N. (2018) 'How Many Millions Have Been Killed in America's Post-9/11 Wars? Part 3: Libya, Syria, Somalia and Yemen'. *Worldbeyondwar.org*. 25 April. Available at https://worldbeyondwar.org/how-many-millions-killed/ (Accessed: 5 September 2019).

Engels, F. (1845) *The Condition of the Working Class in England*. Available at http://marxengels.public-archive.net/en/ME0125en.html (Accessed: 5 September 2019).

Engels, F. (1883) 'Karl Marx's Funeral'. *Der Sozialdemokrat*, 22 March 1883. Available at https://www.marxists.org/archive/marx/works/1883/death/dersoz1.htm (Accessed: 5 September 2019)

Engels, F. (1886) 'Ludwig Feuerbach and the End of Classical German Philosophy'. *Die Neue Zeit*, Issues No. 4 & 5.

Engels, F. (1890) Letter to J. Bloch in Königsberg. Available at https://www.marxists.org/archive/marx/works/1890/letters/90_09_21.htm (Accessed: 5 September 2019).

Engels, F. (1884) *The Origins of the Family, Private Property and the State.* (II. The Family). Available at https://www.marxists.org/archive/marx/works/1884/origin-family/ch02c.htm (Accessed: 5 September 2019).

Gabriel, M. (2011) *Love and Capital: Karl and Jenny Marx and the Birth of a Revolution*. New York: Little, Brown.

Gray, John (2011) 'A Point of View: The Revolution of Capitalism'. *BBC News*, 4 September 2011. https://www.bbc.co.uk/news/magazine-14764357 (Accessed 30 January 2019).

Harvey, D. (2006) *Paris, Capital of Modernity*. London: Routledge.

Jeffries, S. (2012) 'Why Marxism is on the rise again'. *The Guardian*. 4 July. Available at https://www.theguardian.com/world/2012/jul/04/the-return-of-marxism (Accessed: 5 September 2019).

Kapp, Y. (1994) 'Frederick Demuth: new evidence from old sources', *Socialist History*, Vol.6 (1994), pp.17–27.

Krugman, Paul (2009) LSE Lionel Robbins Lecture of 10 June 2009, quoted in *The Economist* http://cep.lse.ac.uk/_new/events/event.asp?id=93

Malandra, Ocean (2017). 'The Irish Potato Famine was Caused by Capitalism, not a Fungus'. *Paste Magazine*, 13 March 2017. www.pastemagazine.com. (Accessed: 2 December 2019).

Marx Memorial Library (2019) 'What can a Marxist approach tell us about racism?'. *Morning Star online*. 25 March. Available at https://morningstaronline.co.uk/article/f/what-can-marxist-approach-tell-us-about-racism (Accessed: 5 September 2019).

McLellan, D. (1983) *Marx*. Glasgow: Fontana.

Neate, R. (2017) 'Richest 1% own half the world' wealth, study finds'. *The Guardian*. 14 November. Available at https://www.theguardian.com/inequality/2017/nov/14/worlds-richest-wealth-credit-suisse (Accessed: 5 September 2019).

Nin, A. (1932) 'The Soviets, their origin, development and function.' *Libcom.org*. Available at https://libcom.org/library/soviets-their-origin-development-functions-andreu-nin (Accessed: 5 September 2019).

Sainato, M. (2019) '"We are not robots": Amazon employees push to unionize'. *The Guardian*. 1 January. Available at https://www.theguardian.com/technology/2019/jan/01/amazon-fulfillment-center-warehouse-employees-union-new-york-minnesota (Accessed: 5 September 2019).

Stedman Jones, Gareth. (2016) *Karl Marx: Greatness and Illusion*. London: Allen Lane.

Tims, P.V. (2018) 'Culture Punch: the BBC's right wing bias'. *Culture Matters*. 2 December. Available at https://culturematters.org.uk/index.php/culture/tv/item/2947-culture-punch-the-bbc-s-right-wing-bias (Accessed: 5 September 2019).

Wheen, F. (1999) *Karl Marx*. London: Fourth Estate.

Wheen, F. (2005) 'Why Marx is man of the moment'. *The Guardian*. 17 July 2005. Available at https://www.theguardian.com/politics/2005/jul/17/comment.theobserver1 (Accessed: 5 September 2019).

Woodcock, A. (2019) 'Austerity has cut UK GDP growth by almost £100bn'. *The Independent*, 21 February 2019. Available at https://www.independent.co.uk/news/business/news/austerity-uk-gdp-growth-tax-economy-chancellor-philip-hammond-a8789866.html (Accessed: 3 December 2019).

Woods, A. (2009) 'Spartacus: a real representative of the proletariat of ancient times'. *In Defence of Marxism*. 3 April. Available at https://www.marxist.com/spartacus-representative-of-proletariat.htm (Accessed: 5 September 2019).

Biography

Manus McGrogan is a historian and author on the May 1968 events in France and their legacy, and more broadly of the global radical movements of the 1960s and 70s. His interest in Marx stems from socialist and antiwar activism. A trained languages and history lecturer, McGrogan has taught in both secondary and higher education, most recently at the Universities of Portsmouth and Sussex. Originally from Belfast, he has lived in Brighton since 1983.

Acknowledgements

Thanks to Isabel Hollands for her initial encouragement in my starting this book. I am much obliged to Sarah Tomley, who was a conscientious mentor in the writing and editing process. Kudos to Dr Ron Haas of Texas State University, who was my avid interlocutor and commentator on Marx in the latter stages of writing. And finally, thanks to comrades and reviewers Brian Parkin and Judy Cox.

Dedication

In memory of Leon Trotsky

Picture Credits:

Fig. 1 'Jenny von Westphalen, date unknown'Unknown (https://commons.wikimedia.org/wiki/File:Jenny_Marx_photograph.jpg), 'Jenny Marx photograph', marked as public domain, more details on Wikimedia Commons: https://commons.wikimedia.org/wiki/Template:PD-1923. **Fig. 2** 'Marx and Engels at the Rheinische Zeitung, 1849', E. Capiro (https://commons.wikimedia.org/wiki/File:Marx_and_Engels_at_the_Rheinische_Zeitung.jpg), 'Marx and Engels at the Rheinische Zeitung', marked as public domain, more details on Wikimedia Commons: https://commons.wikimedia.org/wiki/Template:PD-old. **Fig. 3** 'Karl Marx, 1861', Richard Beard (https://commons.wikimedia.org/wiki/File:Marx4.jpg), 'Marx4', marked as public domain, more details on Wikimedia Commons: https://commons.wikimedia.org/wiki/Template:PD-1923. **Fig. 4** 'Cartoon by Friedrich Engels of Die Freien, the Berlin section of the Young Hegelians, c. 1842', Friedrich Engels (https://commons.wikimedia.org/wiki/File:Die_Freien_by_Friedrich_Engels.jpg), 'Die Freien by Friedrich Engels', marked as public domain, more details on Wikimedia Commons: https://commons.wikimedia.org/wiki/Template:PD-1923.**Fig. 5** 'Friedrich Engels, 1879', Unknown (https://commons.wikimedia.org/wiki/File:Friedrich_Engels_portrait_(cropped).jpg), 'Friedrich Engels portrait (cropped)', marked as public domain, more details on Wikimedia Commons: https://commons.wikimedia.org/wiki/Template:PD-1923. **Fig. 6** 'Luddites smashing textile looms which were causing falling wages and unemployment.' Chris Sunde; original uploader was Christopher Sunde at en.wikipedia. (https://commons.wikimedia.org/wiki/File:FrameBreaking-1812.jpg), 'FrameBreaking-1812', marked as public domain, more details on Wikimedia Commons: https://commons.wikimedia.org/wiki/Template:PD-old. **Fig. 7** 'The Communist Manifesto, 1847', Karl Marx (https://commons.wikimedia.org/wiki/File:Iishmarx.jpg), 'Iishmarx', marked as public domain, more details on Wikimedia Commons: https://commons.wikimedia.org/wiki/Template:PD-old. **Fig 8** 'A caricature by Ferdinand Schröder on the defeat of the revolutions of 1848/49 in Europe' (published in Düsseldorfer Monatshefte, August 1849.) Ferdinand Schröder creator QS:P170,Q1405787 (https://commons.wikimedia.org/wiki/File:Rundgemälde_Europa_1849.jpg), 'Rundgemälde Europa 1849', marked as public domain, more details on Wikimedia Commons: https://commons.wikimedia.org/wiki/Template:PD-old. **Fig. 9** 'Pyramid of Capitalist System', Industrial Workers of the World (IWW) poster printed in 1911. Pyramid of Capitalist System, issued by Nedeljkovich, Brashich, and Kuharich in 1911. Published by The International Pub. Co. , Cleveland OH.IWW (https://commons.wikimedia.org/wiki/File:Anti-capitalism_color.jpg), 'Anti-capitalism color', marked as public domain, more details on Wikimedia Commons: https://commons.wikimedia.org/wiki/Template:PD-US. **Fig. 10** Franco-Prussian War, Strasbourg, 15 October 1870. Original drawing by William Simpson (1823-1899) redrawn by Arthur Hopkins (1848-1930). (https://commons.wikimedia.org/wiki/File:Franco-Prussian_War_-_Strausbourg_-_October_15_1870_-_right003.PNG), 'Franco-Prussian War - Strausbourg - October 15 1870 - right003', marked as public domain, more details on Wikimedia Commons: https://commons.wikimedia.org/wiki/Template:PD-old. **Fig. 11** 'Makeshift barricades are constructed by the Paris Commune to keep out the French Army during La Semaine Sanglante (Bloody Week), 1871', Franck artist QS:P170,Q5868307 (https://commons.wikimedia.org/wiki/File:Franck,_Colonne_Vendôme,_1871.jpg), 'Franck, Colonne Vendôme, 1871', https://creativecommons.org/publicdomain/zero/1.0/legalcode

Printed in Great Britain
by Amazon

18545029R00072